ONTARIO PREHISTORY

Commission archéologique
du Canada
Musée national de l'Homme

Archæological Survey of Canada
National Museum of Man

Publié par les
Musées nationaux du Canada

Published by the
National Museums of Canada

Rédaction
Jacqueline Cernat

Copy editor
Jacqueline Cernat

Coordination
Merle Storey

Project editor
Merle Storey

Direction
Norman J. Boudreau

Managing editor
Norman J. Boudreau

Graphisme
Luc Lymburner

Designer
Luc Lymburner

Ouvrage subventionné par
Le Fonds Margaret Hess
d'Études canadiennes
du Musée national de l'Homme

Publication supported by
The Margaret Hess
Canadian Studies Fund
of the National Museum of Man

ONTARIO PREHISTORY

an eleven-thousand-year
archæological outline

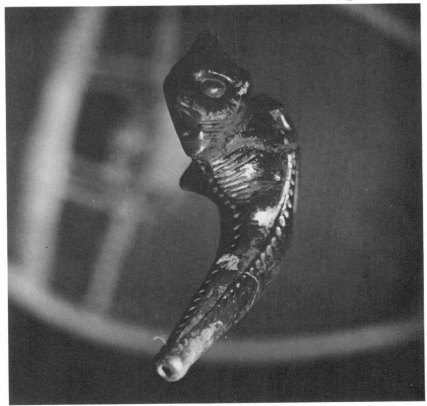

J. V. WRIGHT

OTTAWA 1972

archæological survey of canada
NATIONAL MUSEUM OF MAN

NATIONAL MUSEUMS OF CANADA

Photographs: Photography Division,
National Museums of Canada

Cover: Pinched-face Huron effigy pipe
and Algonkin snowshoe (background)

These two objects symbolize the two
native language families of Ontario
which dominated the province for
many thousands of years.

Available by mail from the
National Museums of Canada
Marketing Services
Ottawa K1A OM8

Catalogue No. NM 92-3772

National Museum of Man
National Museums of Canada
Ottawa, Canada
Second quarter, 1972

PO987654321
Y798765432
Litho in Canada

contents

list of illustrations

résumé

Depuis 70 ans, les fouilles
archéologiques ont mis à découvert une
riche préhistoire, retraçant les origines,
les caractéristiques et le mode de vie
des premiers habitants de l'Ontario.

La préhistoire de la province se divise en
quatre périodes principales: de 9000 à
5000 av. J.-C., la période paléo-indienne;
de 5000 à 1000 av. J.-C., la période
archaïque; de 1000 av. J.-C. à 1000 apr.
J.-C., la période Woodland initiale; et de
1000 apr. J.-C. à la période historique,
la période Woodland terminale.

Des recherches intéressantes sont
prévues mais elles sont sérieusement
menacées par le progrès industriel et
urbain. Le public est invité à protéger le
patrimoine préhistorique de l'Ontario,
avant qu'il ne soit irrévocablement
perdu.

summary

Archæological research in Ontario during the last 70 years has brought to light extensive information about the origins, traits and life styles of the province's earlier inhabitants.

The prehistory of Ontario is divided into four main periods: the Palæo-Indian period, 9000-5000 B.C.; the Archaic period, 5000-1000 B.C.; the Initial Woodland period, 1000 B.C.-1000 A.D.; and the Terminal Woodland period, 1000 A.D. to the Historic period.

Future research in Ontario holds great promise. However, it is seriously threatened by urban and industrial development. Public concern is urged for the protection of the province's archæological heritage.

SOUTHERN ONTARIO

HURON-PETUN-NEUTRAL-ERIE (DESTROYED 1649 A.D.-1654 A.D.)   ST. LAWRENCE IROQUOIS (DESTROYED 1550 A.D.)

ONTARIO IROQUOIS CULTURES

LARGE PALISADED VILLAGES

CORN AGRICULTURE (POPULATION EXPLOSION)

BEANS

OSSUARY BURIAL

PRINCESS POINT CULTURE

INFLUENCES FROM HOPEWELLIAN CULTURE (BURIAL MOUNDS ALONG SOUTHERN MARGIN)

WIDENING TRADE RELATIONS (SHELL, COPPER, SILVER, EXOTIC FLINTS) SMOKING PIPE

SAUGEEN-POINT PENINSULA MEADOWOOD CULTURES

———————— INTRODUCTION OF POTTERY ————————

LAURENTIAN CULTURE

(FIRST APPEARANCE OF POLISHED STONE AND COPPER TOOLS)

DOG BURIAL

VILLAGE CEMETERIES

PLANO CULTURE

(WEAKLY REPRESENTED AND SHARED AREA WITH CLOVIS CULTURE DESCENDANTS)

CLOVIS CULTURE

(EARLIEST EVIDENCE OF MAN IN THE PROVINCE)

YEARS AGO	PERIOD
250	TERMINAL WOODLAND
1000	
2000	INITIAL WOODLAND
3000	
4000	ARCHAIC
5000	
6000	
7000	
8000	PALAEO-INDIAN
9000	
10000	

Diagram 1. Illustrated chronological chart.

FIGURES	
	ALGONKIANS (NATIVE TOOLS REPLACED BY EUROPEAN SUBSTITUTES)

ALGONKIAN CULTURE

DOG BURIAL

LAUREL CULTURE

MARGINAL INFLUENCES FROM HOPEWELLIAN CULTURE (BURIAL MOUNDS)

INTRODUCTION OF POTTERY

SHIELD CULTURE

(EVOLVING OUT OF PLANO CULTURE — FIRST APPEARANCE OF COPPER TOOLS)

PLANO CULTURE

(RESTRICTED TO THE SOUTHERN MARGIN OF THE REGION)

CREMATION BURIAL

VIRTUALLY ALL OF NORTHERN ONTARIO COVERED BY THE CONTINENTAL GLACIER AND ASSOCIATED GLACIAL LAKES

preface

This book is written for the general public and its main purpose is to provide an outline of the prehistoric events that have taken place in the province of Ontario over the last 11,000 years. Technical terms and concepts have been avoided in order that as many interested people as possible may have access to the knowledge that has been acquired by archæologists working in the province during the past 70 years.

In attempting to present a general picture of Ontario's prehistory, it has been necessary to make the complex appear simple, the poorly known appear well known, and to favour one interpretation when, in fact, several conflicting interpretations exist. As such, the following reconstruction will obviously reflect the writer's personal view of what happened in Ontario prior to the arrival of the Europeans in the seventeenth century. Despite this unavoidable bias I believe that most archæologists will be in essential agreement with the major themes of the outline.

Archæology is a discipline that attempts to reconstruct human events and developments that took place prior to written records. Samuel de Champlain was able to make many valuable observations concerning the Hurons with whom he wintered in 1615-1616 A.D., but he was unable to comment on where the Hurons originally came from, how they learned to plant corn, beans, and squash, and when they first began smoking tobacco. The how, why, when, and where of the unknown past are the questions that must, for the most part, be answered by archæology. To achieve its ends, archæology has developed a wide range of field and laboratory techniques which permit the reconstruction of past cultures. Granted, most of these reconstructions are rough frameworks; but they are continuously being built upon, modified, and in general refined.

The vast bulk of the material being analyzed consists of such things as broken tools and food bones, and in a very real sense archæologists are glorified collectors and analyzers of prehistoric garbage. Unfortunately most of the culture that the archæologist is attempting to reconstruct has disappeared a long time ago. If you look around the room in which you are now reading and exclude everything except glass, china, brick, and a few other imperishable objects, you will have some idea how little the archæologists of the future will have to work with in terms of our own culture. Despite these limitations, sufficient information survives the ravages of time and nature to allow the archæologist to at least partially decipher the past. Different prehistoric cultures made different stone and bone tools, built their houses and buried their dead in different ways. Some were hunters and others were farmers, some made pottery vessels and others did not. It is this host of similarities and differences that permits the archæologist to establish various prehistoric cultural groups and to trace their development through time.

In writing about prehistoric cultures, archæologists usually begin with the earliest known groups and advance towards the late or historic period. The reason for going from early to late is probably related to the fact that in so doing we progress from the simple (more ignorance) to the complex (less ignorance). During the actual mechanics of establishing his sequences, however, the archæologist often begins with the historic period and works his way progressively further back into prehistoric times. This technique is referred to as the direct historical approach which simply consists of working from the known to the unknown.

Historic villages, documented by early explorers and missionaries, are located and authenticated by the presence of European trade goods and other evidence. The native artifacts of pottery, stone, and bone associated with the European artifacts are then compared to a nearby site not containing European artifacts and if the comparisons are close then it is assumed that the latter site was occupied by the ancestors of the people who lived in the historic site. The artifacts and other evidence from the prehistoric village are then compared with other prehistoric villages and on the assumption that the degree of similarity reflects a relationship in time, it is possible to extend a series of site relationships down through time with the identified historic sites as a starting point. This sequence of sites is taken to represent the prehistoric development of the culture or tribe identified by the historic sources. The great value of this approach is that it allows the archæologist to make more meaningful cultural reconstructions by drawing from the historic, ethnological, and linguistic sources, cultural data that otherwise could not possibly be provided by the limited remains of prehistoric sites. As archæology is one of the disciplines of the larger field of anthropology, it is only reasonable that the archæologist, as a specialized anthropologist, attempt to provide some flesh from the living areas of anthropology to clothe the lean prehistoric skeleton that he has been able to create, using certain special techniques.

In order to recreate history from the fragmented and vague evidence left by prehistoric man, the archæologist must be a jack of all trades. He must know sufficient geology to separate man's work from that of nature, to identify varieties of stone, and interpret the manner of soil deposition and modification. He must know sufficient biology to identify and interpret animal and plant remains. He must know some chemistry, physics, mathematics and a range of other disciplines that will assist him in his work.

Above everything else, however, he must attempt to know and understand man. The broken tools and other items found around an ancient camp fire are only garbage. The vague outlines of ancient houses and other features are only ghostly reflections of what has been. But all of these things are the products of man—man with his infinite variety and complexity. Man has always been fascinated by himself and, therefore, it is only natural that some men will attempt to understand the past. It is man's nature to acquire knowledge but some might say, "What earthly use is knowledge of the past?" There are a number of answers to this question, one of which may be taken from an ancient Chinese story which runs roughly like this:

On top of a high hill sits a lone philosopher contemplating nature. At the base of the hill a long caravan loaded with goods winds its way towards the city. The merchant heading the caravan notices the solitary figure on top of the hill and walks up to him saying,

"Why do you waste your time contemplating nature? Why do you not do as I and acquire wealth and prestige?''

The philosopher then asked the merchant, ''You would say that anything that is not of direct and immediate use is, therefore, useless?''

Upon the merchant replying ''Yes,'' the philosopher continued, ''Is it not true that when you walked up the hill you only needed the soil your foot trod upon?''

''Yes.''

''If everything else was removed and only pillars of earth sufficient for your path remained, then this would be adequate for your purposes?''

''Yes.''

''Would you care to live in such a world?''

Until recently archæological research in Ontario was carried on the shoulders of two or three men. There are now more than 12 archæologists working either full time or part time in the province. In addition, there are a number of very competent non-professionals who have made substantial contributions to the province's prehistory. There is also a provincial archæological society that publishes a journal, holds meetings, undertakes excavations, and is involved in the province's prehistory in a number of ways. Indeed, archæology is a fortunate discipline in that non-professionals can play an active and productive role when they work in close accord with professionals. Finally, there are a number of graduate students who are excavating sites in the summer and analyzing the recovered data in the winter.

The markedly increased tempo of archæological investigation has produced a number of books and papers, the vast majority of which are quite technical. Such technical publications, however, are the building blocks of any general statement intended for the public. It is a credit to the amount and quality of the archæological work done in the province that a general synthesis can even be attempted. Certainly, less than ten years ago such an attempt would have been impossible.

acknowledgments

To acknowledge all the people and institutions that have directly or indirectly contributed to this book would undoubtedly result in a work half again as large. Many contributors will never be known: interested citizens who have donated specimens and/or information; politicians and civil servants who have provided and expanded financial and material support for archæological exploration and analysis; and a host of individuals, in various walks of life, who have worked in a multitude of ways to preserve and increase the knowledge of the province of Ontario's prehistoric heritage.

The written contributions are acknowledged in the Suggested Reading List at the end of the book. In a very real sense, however, these published works represent the tip of an iceberg. The bulk of the available archæological information on Ontario's prehistory still resides in unpublished monographs, notes, partially analyzed collections of artifacts, and the heads of many individuals.

In addition to a general expression of appreciation to the many individuals who have made this book possible, I would like to acknowledge my debt to the institution that has supported my research for more than a decade—the National Museum of Man. More specifically, I thank two members of the Archæology Division staff: Mr. J. A. Dellaire, Custodian of Collections, for innumerable services rendered over the years; and Mr. D. W. Laverie, Draftsman, for the excellent maps and drawings.

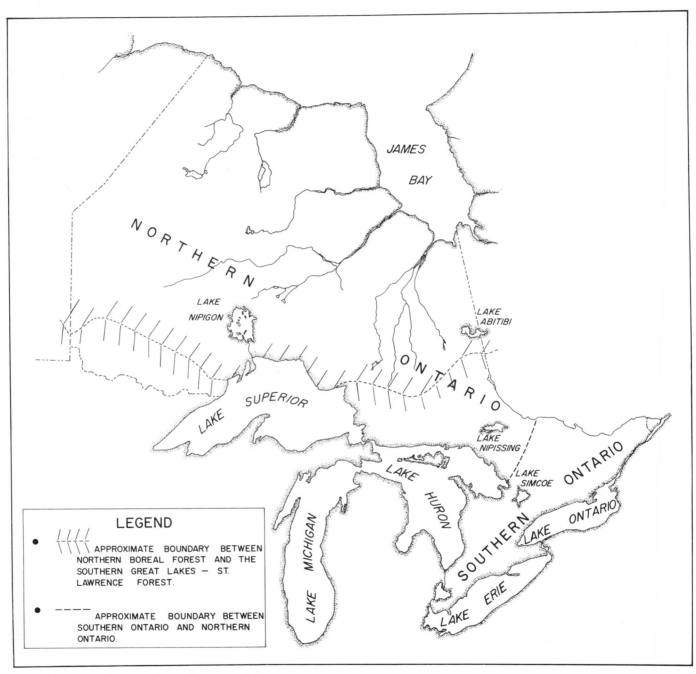

Map 1. Northern and Southern Regions of Ontario.

Introduction

The Northern and Southern Regions and Archæological Periods

The prehistory of the Indians who occupied Ontario can best be understood by dividing the province into two major regions—a Northern region and a Southern region. Most of the Northern region is within the Canadian Shield and has a predominantly coniferous forest, whereas the Southern region has a predominantly hardwood forest.

It is not completely by accident that the archæological division of the province is essentially the same as the political division, with Northern Ontario being composed of districts and Southern Ontario consisting of counties. The more kindly endowed Southern region has always supported a far greater prehistoric population than the harsh Northern region and the same situation exists today with reference to modern population densities. The richer archæology of the south, however, has been complicated by the development of local cultural groups which interacted with each other and outside areas in a highly complex fashion. On the other hand, the Northern region is characterized by a high degree of cultural similarity which allows certain general interpretations to be drawn from relatively limited archæological data. The available evidence suggests that the prehistory of these two regions or culture areas has been distinct and different from the earliest beginnings to the historic period. Certainly cultural interactions and contacts took place along a broad span of the somewhat ill-defined boundary between the two areas but such events appear to have been relatively unimportant.

The prehistory of Ontario will be considered under four periods: the Palæo-Indian period (9000 B.C.-5000 B.C.), the Archaic period (5000 B.C.-1000 B.C.), the Initial Woodland period (1000 B.C.-1000 A.D.), and the Terminal Woodland period (1000 A.D.-to the historic period). This last period ends shortly after the appearance of the French and the English who introduce the historic period.

In many respects the four periods are artificial devices created by the archæologist to assist his study of the approximately 11,000 years of Ontario prehistory. It would be very convenient to be able to slice up the time column into four layers which could then be described as separate entities but, in truth, matters are not that simple and there are very fuzzy areas between and within these major periods. Each period, however, does possess certain characteristics which differentiate it from the other periods.

ONTARIO PREHISTORY

YEARS AGO	PERIOD	SOUTHERN ONTARIO	NORTHERN ONTARIO
250	TERMINAL WOODLAND	ONTARIO IROQUOIS AND ST. LAWRENCE IROQUOIS CULTURES	ALGONKIAN CULTURE
1000			
2000	INITIAL WOODLAND	PRINCESS POINT CULTURE SAUGEEN-POINT PENINSULA - MEADOWOOD CULTURES	LAUREL CULTURE
3000			
4000	ARCHAIC	LAURENTIAN CULTURE	SHIELD CULTURE
5000			
6000			
7000	PALAEO — INDIAN		PLANO CULTURE
8000		PLANO CULTURE	
9000			
10,000		CLOVIS CULTURE	
11,000			

Diagram 2. Chronological chart.

I. the palaeo-indian period

(ca. 9000 B.C.- 5000 B.C.)

Map 2. The Palaeo-Indian period. The extent of both the Continental Ice Sheet and Glacial Lake Agassiz pertains only to their locations 11,000 years ago. Both before and after this date the dimensions of the Continental Glacier and its associated glacial lakes were markedly different. For example, as Lake Agassiz shrank in size the Plano people moved into the area of the former lake bed and lost the dart heads that are plotted on the map.

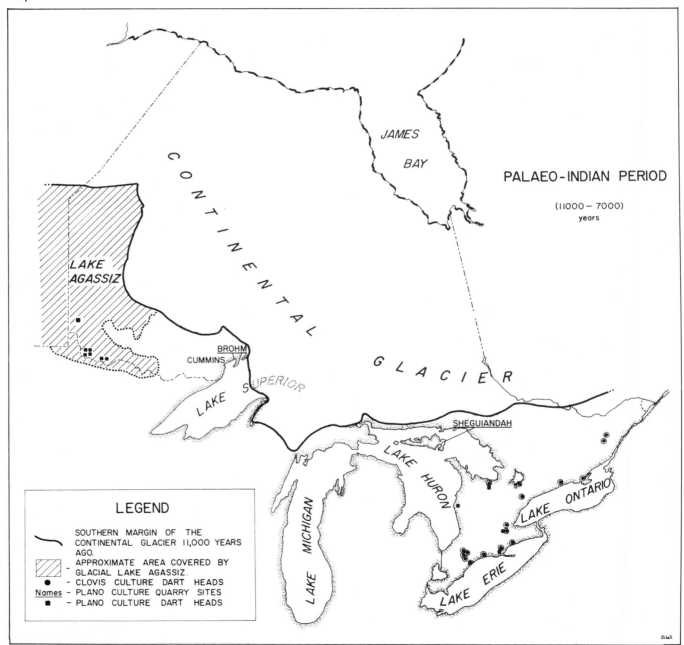

JAMES BAY

PALAEO-INDIAN PERIOD

(11000 – 7000) years

CONTINENTAL

GLACIER

LAKE AGASSIZ

BROHM
CUMMINS

LAKE SUPERIOR

SHEGUIANDAH

LAKE HURON

LAKE MICHIGAN

LAKE ONTARIO

LAKE ERIE

LEGEND

SOUTHERN MARGIN OF THE CONTINENTAL GLACIER 11,000 YEARS AGO.
APPROXIMATE AREA COVERED BY GLACIAL LAKE AGASSIZ.
● – CLOVIS CULTURE DART HEADS
Names – PLANO CULTURE QUARRY SITES
■ – PLANO CULTURE DART HEADS

Fig. 1. Clovis culture dart heads.

I. The Palaeo-Indian Period (ca. 9000 B.C.-5000 B.C.)

The Palæo-Indian period is represented by two cultures that possessed distinctively different tools but followed a basically similar way of life. The earlier culture is called Clovis and appears to have been ancestral to the later culture called Plano.

Clovis culture

Clovis culture is found throughout most of North America east of the Rocky Mountains except, of course, for those areas that were still covered by the continental glacier. Although no Clovis culture sites have yet been discovered in Ontario a number of the stone dart heads characteristic of the culture have been found throughout the southern portion of the province. Further penetration to the north, however, was effectively stopped by the continental ice sheet. The climate along this ice front 11,000 to 10,000 years ago appears to have been subarctic and it is most likely that the major prey of these early hunters was the caribou. There is the likelihood too that such extinct late Pleistocene mammals as the mammoth and mastodon were also hunted.

The ancestors of the Clovis culture entered North America from Asia at a time when the two continents were connected by a broad plain. Indeed, they would probably have been ignorant of the fact that they were occupying another continent. To judge by the uniformity of their culture, these big game hunters from Asia must have spread very rapidly throughout most of North America.

Until very recently, it was held by most archæologists that the Clovis people were the first immigrants to the New World and that their rapid spread was due to the superabundance of game animals and the absence of competition

Colour Plate I. Late Laurentian Archaic grave goods (1500 B.C.-1000 B.C.) from cemeteries in the Picton area, eastern Lake Ontario.

With few exceptions prehistoric trade was closely associated with religious beliefs and the trade objects are generally recovered from graves as objects intended to accompany the spirit of the dead to the after life. Powdered red ochre and a specially prepared green clay are also common occurrences in graves of this period. As can be seen in the illustration, the red ochre still adheres to a number of the artifacts.

The shell pendants and beads are all manufactured from the Conch shell which would have originally come from the Gulf of Mexico nearly 1,000 miles to the south. The large pendant in the upper left-hand corner had been broken and subsequently repaired by drilling a series of lashing holes. The native copper celts and awls are made from Lake Superior copper. For reasons that will never be known the celts generally occur in pairs. The galena chunks (lead sulphide) in the lower left-hand corner probably came from Morris Island near Arnprior on the Ottawa River.

Trade in these objects almost certainly involved multiple hand-to-hand transactions rather than actual trading parties traversing the enormous areas involved.

from earlier human occupants. New evidence from an unglaciated portion of the Yukon Territory now strongly suggests that man was present 25,000 to 30,000 years ago and, possibly, much earlier. Supporting evidence further to the south, however, is still somewhat vague. In the light of this new information, it now appears that the Clovis culture must have either overrun and absorbed an earlier population or, in an unknown fashion, it must be descended from the earlier people. Possibly some of these earlier people may have been forced further south to form the early cultures of South America which are distinctively different from Clovis culture, yet of approximately the same antiquity. After spreading rapidly throughout most of North America, the Clovis culture settled down and gradually changed in response to local conditions and increasing population densities.

The host of local cultures that developed from the relatively homogeneous Clovis culture base can be broadly divided into a western group and an eastern group. Consideration of the eastern group is given in the chapter on the Archaic period.

Plano culture

The western group—the Plano cultures—developed, for the most part, on the high plains and their penetration into the east was very incomplete. In the southwestern area of Northern Ontario occasional finds of dart heads, which have been dated approximately 9,000 years at sites further to the west, have been made. Many of these stone projectile points exhibit the fine "ripple" flaking that is one of the major markers of the Plano cultures. Along the north shores of Lake Superior and on Manitoulin Island in Lake Huron quarries worked by Plano people have been found. These quarries are in deposits of high quality siliceous stone such as taconite and quartzite, the raw materials from which the early hunters made their stone tools. Such sites are characteristically littered with flakes, cores, and unfinished tools broken or discarded during an early stage of the manufacturing process. Some sites, such as the Sheguiandah site on Manitoulin Island, had been used by various people for over 10,000 years. Other quarry sites, such as the ones near Thunder Bay, had been exploited only by Plano people. The latter sites, which were originally on the shoreline, are now as much as six miles inland and nearly 200 feet above the

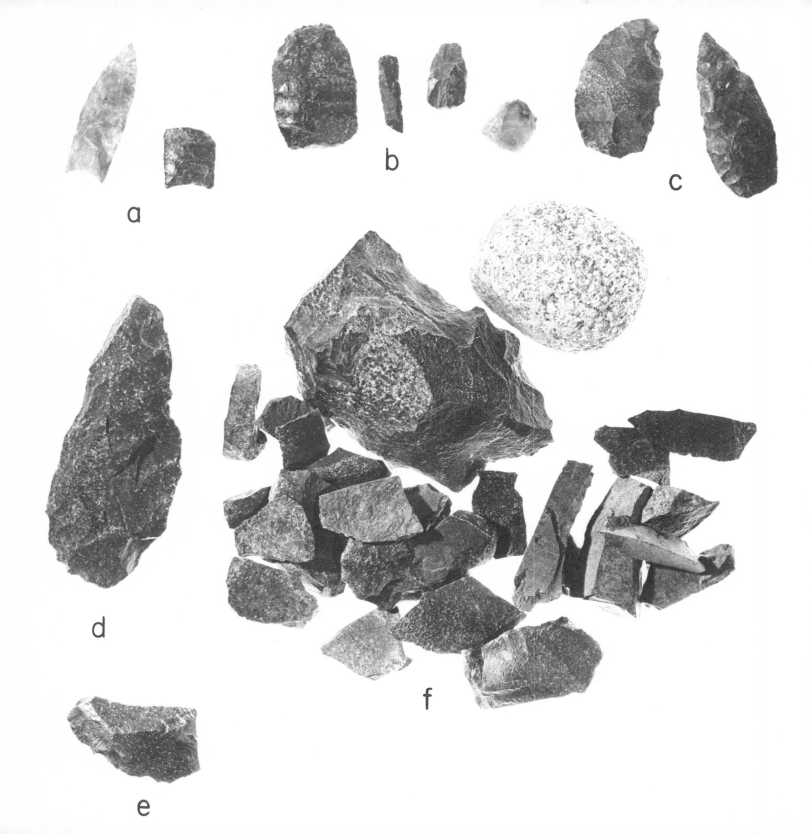

a

b

c

d

e

f

Plate 1. Plano Culture artifacts.

Fig. a. Typical dart heads.

Fig. b. A range of scraping tools that would have been used to fashion wood and bone as well as scrape hides and cut sinews.

Fig. c. Knives.

Fig. d. A crudely fashioned block of stone called a preform. Such items, which were eventually worked into dart heads, knives, and other tools, represent an early stage of stone tool manufacture.

Fig. e. Specialized tool used for slotting bone and wood.

Fig. f. Hammerstone, large core, and flakes typical of quarry sites where the siliceous deposits of taconite, quartzite or flint were fashioned through a series of stages into finished or semi-finished implements.

Plate 2. Quarry pit at the Sheguiandah site, Manitoulin Island, used throughout the Palæo-Indian and Archaic periods. Excavation of this relatively small quarry pit revealed that the ancient miners had excavated through solid, fine-grained quartzite bedrock to a depth of 4 feet using only large stone hammers. The stone fragments surrounding the archæological excavation are flakes, cores, and implements broken during the manufacturing process.

present lake level. An archæologist must know something about the local geological events that altered lake levels and land surfaces if he hopes to discover these early sites. In addition to the preceding sites a few typical Plano projectile points have been picked up from fields in Southern Ontario, particularly in the western region. Since all but the marginal areas of Northern Ontario were still covered by the glacier between 9,500 and 8,500 years ago, evidence of Plano culture in these areas is, of course, lacking.

The Clovis and the Plano cultures are the products of hunting peoples who exploited large game animals. We can assume that they had developed clothing and shelter to a degree that allowed them to survive under severe climatic conditions. The information that we possess on the Palæo-Indian period in Ontario, however, is very limited. At this early time period we are certainly dealing with very sparse populations. Further, the country they occupied was substantially different physio-

graphically (climate, flora, fauna, bodies of water and drainages) than it is today. These differences, which were a direct product of the proximity of the continental glacier, make it extremely difficult to locate sites that can be excavated by the archæologist. Time and acid soils have both combined to destroy all tools made from substances other than stone. With very few exceptions the archæologist must attempt to reconstruct the Palæo-Indian period in Ontario from the discarded, broken, and lost stone projectile points, knives, scrapers, and other tools. Rarely, such as occurred at one of the Plano sites on the north shore of Lake Superior, features representing a pit and a cremation burial are encountered.

Sufficient information has survived the ravages of time, however, to demonstrate that for the approximately 4,000 years of the Palæo-Indian period, habitable portions of the province were occupied by man and that these first occupants laid the ground work for subsequent developments.

Colour Plate II. Late Shield Archaic (1500 B.C.) grave goods from a richly endowed grave to the south of Lake Nipigon.

Only the native copper and stone objects have survived the passage of time and the acid soils. Copper objects are represented by the following: socketed dart and lance heads, socketed knives, awls, chisels, punches, bossed bracelets, disc pendants, hammered nodules representing the beginning stage of manufacture into implements, and objects whose functions are unknown. Stone implements include dart heads, knives, and a wide variety of scrapers. Some of the scrapers and the knife in the lower left-hand corner are manufactured from a distinctive flint found in North Dakota. Red ochre in powdered form also occurred in the grave.

The religious ideas suggested in this Shield Archaic grave appear to have originated in the mid-western states and to have been introduced to the northerners.

II. the archaic period

(ca. 5000 B.C.-1000 B.C.)

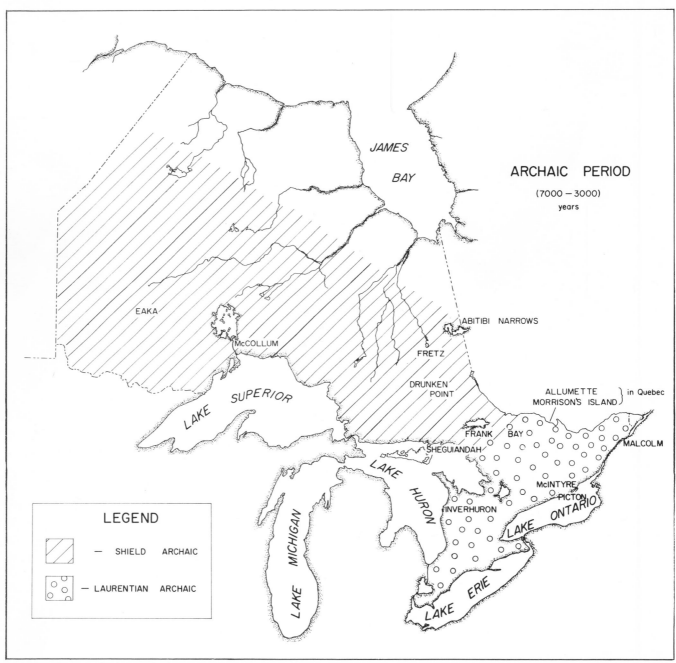

Map 3. The Archaic period.

LEGEND

▨ — SHIELD ARCHAIC

⊡ — LAURENTIAN ARCHAIC

ARCHAIC PERIOD

(7000 – 3000) years

JAMES BAY

EAKA

McCOLLUM

ABITIBI NARROWS

FRETZ

DRUNKEN POINT

ALLUMETTE } in Quebec
MORRISON'S ISLAND

MALCOLM

LAKE SUPERIOR

FRANK BAY

SHEGUIANDAH

McINTYRE

PICTON

INVERHURON

LAKE ONTARIO

LAKE HURON

LAKE MICHIGAN

LAKE ERIE

II. The Archaic Period
(ca. 5000 B.C.-1000 B.C.)

Just as the Plano peoples evolved from an earlier Clovis culture base in the west, the early Southern Ontario Archaic peoples appear to have developed out of a similar culture base in the east, but in a significantly different fashion. Although the evidence for the development of Archaic out of Clovis comes mainly from the southeastern United States, similar as yet undiscovered developments probably took place further to the north. The early appearance of Archaic peoples in the east also probably accounts for the incomplete eastern penetration of the Plano peoples of the late Palæo-Indian period. It now appears that when the eastward drift of the Plano hunters began, the east was already occupied by indigenous people; in a number of sites found in the upper Great Lakes, Plano and early Archaic tools occur in direct association.

The very simplified Diagram 3 should be of assistance in understanding the ancestral role of Clovis culture to both the Plano culture of the west and the Archaic culture of the east.

While the sparse Clovis population of Southern Ontario probably contributed to the subsequent Archaic cultures, a large number of ideas, technologies, and people apparently immigrated into the area. Ground slate lances and projectile points appear to have been introduced from the east. The knowledge necessary for producing tools and ornaments from native copper came from the west and the distinctive stone weights used to increase the efficiency of the spear thrower originated in the south. Tools such as the gouge (a specialized polished stone adze), certain varieties of chipped stone

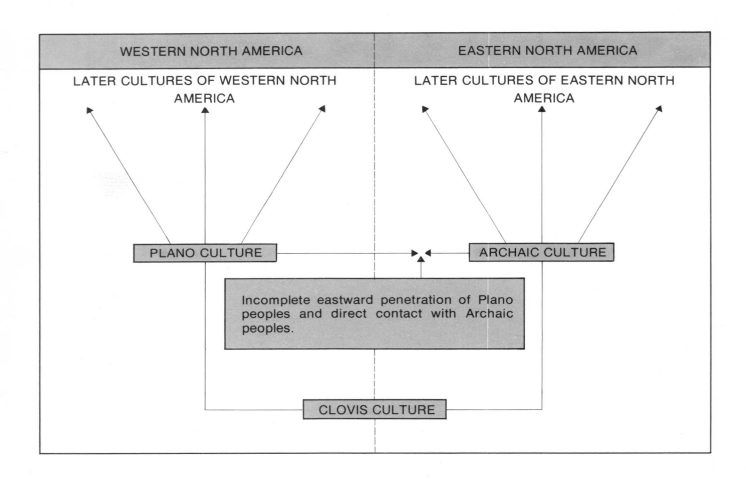

WESTERN NORTH AMERICA	EASTERN NORTH AMERICA
LATER CULTURES OF WESTERN NORTH AMERICA	LATER CULTURES OF EASTERN NORTH AMERICA

PLANO CULTURE

ARCHAIC CULTURE

Incomplete eastward penetration of Plano peoples and direct contact with Archaic peoples.

CLOVIS CULTURE

Diagram 3. Evolution of the Plano and Archaic cultures.

projectile points, and other utilitarian tool varieties may have been developed right in the southern portion of the province.

The earliest beginnings of the Archaic period in Southern Ontario are still poorly known. Beyond a very thin scattering of early projectile point varieties, sometimes associated with late Palæo-Indian period artifacts, we have very little information. Some evidence suggests a penetration into southwestern Southern Ontario by early Archaic hunters from the Ohio Valley via the Windsor area. The first good evidence of a well established Archaic population in Southern Ontario appears about 4000 B.C. and pertains to a culture called the Laurentian Archaic. Closely related people occupied southern Quebec, northern New York and Vermont and more distant cousins are found in the Maritime provinces, Newfoundland and the New England states. The Laurentian Archaic continued to occupy Southern Ontario until the appearance of pottery during the Initial Woodland period.

Plate 4. Archaic dog burial, 1500 B.C.

Laurentian culture

The more than 3,000 years of Laurentian Archaic occupation of Southern Ontario were of paramount importance to the later prehistory of the temperate region of the province. The pattern of life established during this time does not appear to have been significantly altered until the introduction of agriculture. It now appears that the Laurentian people represented the first substantial population of hunters and fishermen to live in Southern Ontario and the way of life that they established was to have a vital impact upon subsequent events.

From the excavation of Laurentian cemeteries in adjacent Quebec and New York, we know that the people were of robust build and suffered to a minor degree accidental fractures, arthritis, and some tooth loss through gum disease. Death by violence is occasionally noted in the form of skull fractures, projectile points lodged in bones or the chest cavity, and decapitation. There is even one recorded instance from New York of unsuccessful surgery to remove a projectile point tip lodged in a human forehead.

An examination of the discarded food bones from sites suggests that the Laurentian people were predominantly big game hunters who relied mainly on such animals as deer, elk, bear, and beaver. Smaller game animals, fish, shell-fish, and wild plant foods were also used but they appear to have supplemented the big game meat diet. This is, of course, a gross generalization and there would certainly have been seasonal rounds when berry picking (late spring through fall depending on species), nut gathering (fall), fishing, passenger pigeon and other migratory bird trapping (spring) were carried out. There would also be the sexual division of labour whereby men would concentrate on big game hunting while women tended the fish nets or gathered wild vegetable foods. For short periods of the year survival might well have depended upon these supplementary food sources, but without the big game animals it is unlikely that the people could have maintained themselves on a year-round basis.

Another variable would be the differences in local resources. For example, an area rich in spring sturgeon would possess an advantage over an area lacking this significant food resource. The latter

a

b

c

d

e

f

g

h

i

Plate 5. Laurentian culture artifacts.

Fig. a. Polished stone gouge. These specialized adzes are characteristic of Laurentian Archaic sites.

Fig. b. Open-socketed native copper dart head.

Fig. c. Polished slate spear-thrower weight. Such counter-weights were attached to the spear-thrower to increase the velocity with which the spear could be propelled. The drilled hole necessary for attachment to the spear-thrower was drilled with a hollow reed used in a bow drill plus a water and sand abrasive.

Fig. d. Ground slate bayonet. Such objects were probably used as the tips of lances.

Fig. e. Stone plummet. Often regarded as sinkers or bola stones, these objects may actually represent specialized pendants.

Fig. f. Ground slate dart head.

Fig. g. Chipped stone drill.

Fig. h. Native copper adze with an open socket for hafting purposes.

Fig. i. Typical dart heads.

Plate 6. Excavation of stratified Archaic site. The black bands in the walls of the excavation represent ancient living floors, with the lowest floor dating at 1700 B.C. and the uppermost floor at 1000 B.C. This particular site on the shore of Lake Huron was a favourite fishing location which was used seasonally by Archaic peoples for many years. Windblown sands off the beach covered each sequential occupation, thus creating the excellent stratification.

area, however, might possess extensive passenger pigeon nesting areas which would offset the absence of the sturgeon spring runs. Such regional variations in available seasonal foodstuffs, plus different geographical positioning relative to outside cultural influences, rapidly resulted in marked regional varieties within the Laurentian Archaic itself.

Southern Ontario, it now appears, can be roughly divided into an eastern variety of Laurentian Archaic and a western variety of Laurentian Archaic, using Toronto as a dividing point.

Nothing is known of the kind of houses that the Laurentian Archaic peoples of Ontario lived in. This is perhaps not too surprising when it is realized that the sites dug by archæologists are summer villages and that flimsy structures may have been used leaving no trace. There is also evidence that 5,000 years ago the warmer climate that then prevailed would have resulted in an extra month of summer, thereby even further reducing the need for substantial houses. In the late fall when the individual families dispersed to their winter hunting grounds, it is very likely that more solid structures were built. Such winter sites, however, would be very small and extremely difficult to locate many thousands of years after they had been abandoned.

The religious beliefs of the Laurentian people are dimly reflected in their methods of burial. Quite early a burial cult developed which involved placing objects for use in the after life with the deceased and sprinkling the body with red ochre. As time went on, the concern with the dead increased and by the end of the Archaic period had reached a peak. Stone, bone, and native copper tools and ornaments were placed with the dead in increasing abundance. Usually, the bodies were stretched straight out on their backs, but occasionally they were flexed and some were cremated. Most of the grave goods were lavished on adult males, suggesting that such individuals held a high status in the society. The dog, man's helper in the hunt, was also buried, generally with adult males.

Some of the grave goods indicate that a wide trading pattern existed. For example, a single grave might contain pendants made from conch shells from the

Plate 7. These ancient hearths, represented by concentrations of fire-cracked rock, have been buried for more than 3,000 years. After being exposed to intensive fire the rocks slowly released their heat and thereby provided an excellent means for slow baking. The shattered rocks resulting from this cooking technique are frequently the first evidence of ancient man that the archæologist encounters. Broken tools and discarded food bones are common in such features.

Gulf of Mexico, shell beads from the Atlantic coast, copper artifacts from Lake Superior, and exotic flints from widely dispersed locales. These items almost certainly arrived in Southern Ontario via many individual hand-to-hand transactions rather than by actual trading parties traversing enormous areas of North America.

Shield culture

At the same time as the Laurentian people were living in Southern Ontario, a quite different Archaic population was living in the harsh lands of Northern Ontario. These people are called the Shield Archaic as their camp sites are found throughout most of the Canadian Shield from Keewatin District in the Northwest Territories to Cape Breton in Nova Scotia. There is evidence that the Shield Archaic people developed out of a late Palæo-Indian period (Plano) culture base

in Keewatin District and probably in Manitoba. As the continental glacier retreated to the east, first plants and then animals, including predators such as man, reoccupied the new territories released by the ice. In this fashion the Shield Archaic people gradually occupied all of Northern Ontario except possibly the Hudson Bay Lowlands which may have been virtually uninhabited until the historic period. Other than the stone tools little has survived the acid soils of the north but sufficient evidence, direct and indirect, exists to attempt a reconstruction of the way of life of the Shield Archaic people.

Despite the lack of bone from Shield Archaic sites, we see that many sites are located at narrows on lakes and rivers that act as natural caribou crossings and there is very little question that the caribou was a key element in the diet of the Shield Archaic people. Fish would also have been important. Indeed, the combination of caribou and fish has probably always been a prerequisite for survival throughout much of the desolate Pre-Cambrian Shield country. Other animals such as bear, beaver, hare, and waterfowl would also have been important as

Plate 8. Shield culture artifacts.

Fig. a. Large core-scraper. Such specimens were first used as cores from which flakes were struck and made into tools. Frequently the core was then retouched along the edges to produce a large, heavy scraping tool.

Fig. b. Scrapers.

Fig. c. Dart heads.

Fig. d. Native copper knife fashioned to include the handle.

Fig. e. Native copper fishhook.

Fig. f. Large stone knives. Very frequently these tools performed a number of functions: scraping faces and graving spurs are chipped into their margins.

Fig. g. Specialized knife typical of the Shield culture where the flaking is largely restricted to a single face.

Fig. h. Lower portion of a large copper gaff. A number of such implements used for gaffing large fish have been recovered from Lake Superior in nets of commercial fishermen.

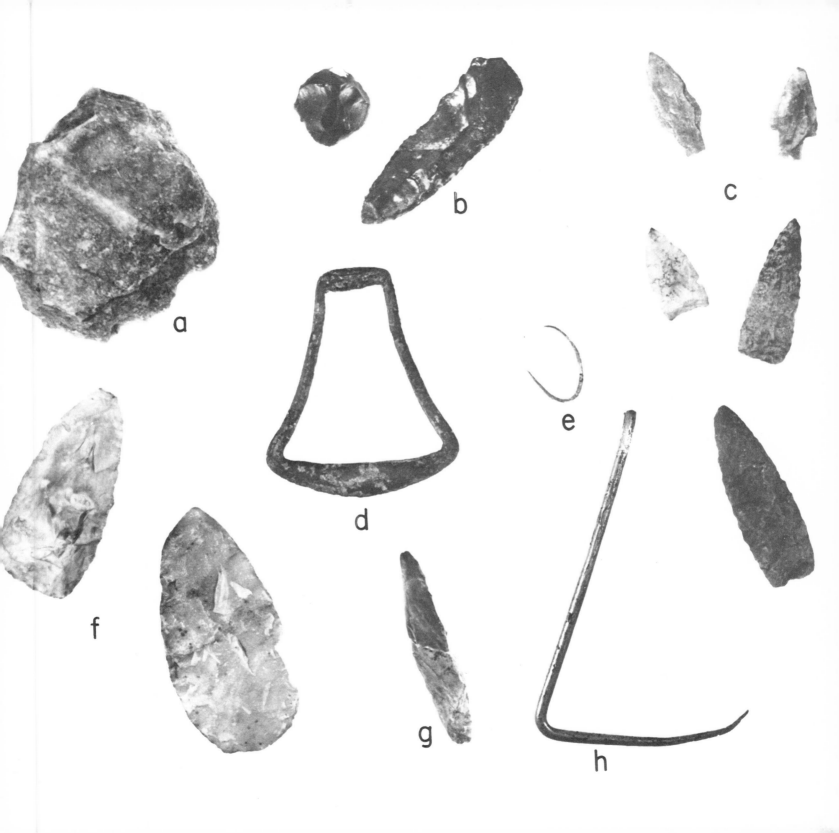

a

b

c

d

e

f

g

h

supplementary or seasonal resources. The new plant growth following the extensive forest fires in the north would have favoured marked increases in the moose population to the point where the moose probably temporarily replaced the caribou in different areas as the major big game animal. Without the presence of caribou and fish, however, it is unlikely that the Shield Archaic peoples could have so completely occupied this extensive and hostile country.

The distribution of sites along the major rivers, interior lakes, and on the islands suggests that these early hunters possessed water craft—probably the birch bark canoe. They must also have known how to manufacture snowshoes, otherwise they could not have survived the heavy snows of winter. It appears that the Shield Archaic people followed a way of life nearly identical to that of the northern Algonkian-speakers of the historic period. They may even have been the ancestors of the historic Cree, Ojibwa, and Algonkin.

We cannot say what the Shield Archaic people looked like for, although a few graves have been discovered, all of the bone has been destroyed by the acid soil. What remains are the stone and copper tools and ornaments, and red ochre placed with the dead. Graves discovered to date are all close to the southern margin of the Shield Archaic territory and many of the burial practices appear to have been borrowed directly from their southern neighbours.

The actual evidence of direct contact between the Shield Archaic and adjacent and contemporaneous peoples, however, is relatively slight. The skills needed to fashion native copper into tools were introduced from eastern Wisconsin. An exotic flint from North Dakota is frequently found on Shield Archaic sites indicating some kind of contact with the prairies. In a broad buffer zone between Northern Ontario and Southern Ontario, Shield Archaic sites frequently contain Laurentian Archaic artifacts, an indication that the two populations were in direct contact. Further into the interior, however, there is slight evidence that the Shield Archaic people were receiving significant outside influence.

III. the woodland period
(ca. 1000 B.C. to Historic Period)

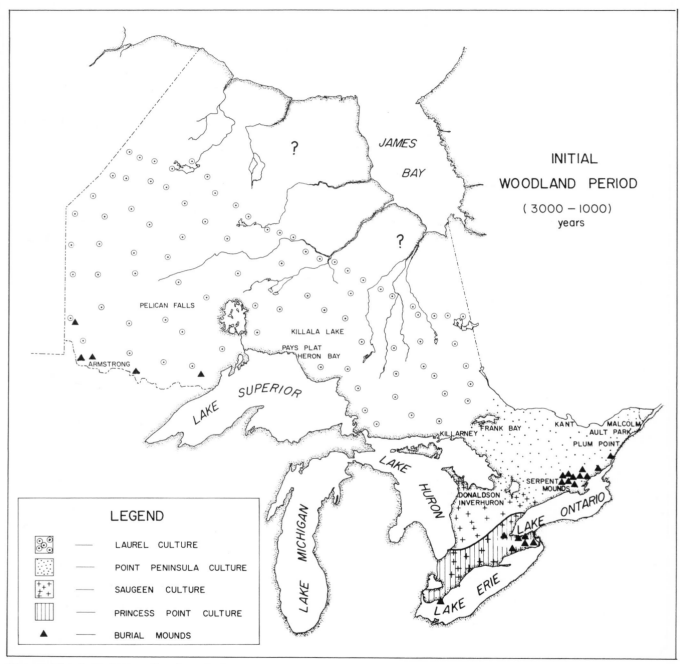

Map 4. The Initial Woodland period.

III. The Woodland Period (ca. 1000 B.C. to Historic Period)

The first appearance of pottery vessels initiates the Woodland period. No great cultural changes take place other than the introduction of a single item—pottery. The appearance of pottery, however, provides the archæologist with a convenient device for dividing the time column into more manageable units. Considerable evidence now exists that the preceding Laurentian and Shield Archaic peoples adopted pottery and were thereby transformed (for the archæologist's convenience) into Woodland peoples. The cultural developments that began with Palæo-Indian through Archaic, however, are unbroken.

Far more is known about the prehistory of the Woodland period than the preceding Archaic and Palæo-Indian periods. We are not only dealing with the products of ever-increasing populations but the ravages of time have had less effect upon the archæological remains. In order to handle conveniently the much increased body of information, the Woodland period has been divided into an Initial Woodland period and a Terminal Woodland period. The Initial Woodland period encompasses those Archaic peoples who first adopted pottery between 700 B.C. and 1000 B.C. and their subsequent descendants up to approximately 1000 A.D. The Terminal Woodland period refers to prehistoric cultures that can be traced by the direct historical approach to historic, documented populations such as the Cree and the Huron. As archæological research progresses the Terminal Woodland period will certainly be pushed further back in time and this artificial 1000 A.D. separating point between the Initial and Terminal Woodland periods will have to be adjusted accordingly.

Some readers might wonder why terms such as "Early," "Middle," and "Late" Woodland have not been used. The reason is simply that these terms have already been used in the archæological literature, often in different and confusing ways. For anyone reading further into the prehistory of Ontario, however, it should be pointed out that the Initial Woodland period equates with the Early Woodland and Middle Woodland periods of the technical literature and that the Terminal Woodland period equates with the Late Woodland period. As knowledge of the prehistory of an area, province, or country expands, the theoretical framework within which this knowledge is organized must also expand and change. This is a painful and confusing adjustment that all disciplines, such as archæology, must undergo periodically.

Colour Plate III. Meadowood culture artifacts.

The function of a number of the diagnostic Meadowood culture artifacts is unknown. Presumably objects such as the birdstone (top), boatstone (far left), and bar amulet (lower left) performed some religious function as they are most frequently encountered in graves. Tobacco-smoking is suggested by the appearance of tubular stone pipes. The specimen at the bottom of the illustration is manufactured from a stone found only in Ohio and is referred to as Ohio pipestone. Large knives or spears such as the one on the right are frequently found in graves and may even have been specifically manufactured for placement with the dead. Ground slate gorgets or pendants, such as the central illustration, also occur in graves.

As may be gathered from the foregoing, most of our information on the Meadowood culture comes from the cemeteries. Small Meadowood culture campsites, howeve., have been recently discovered and when these are excavated and reported upon we can expect to obtain a more complete picture of these little known people.

The Initial Woodland Period (ca. 1000 B.C.-1000 A.D.)

The first appearance of pottery provides the archæologist with a convenient device for terminating the Archaic period and introducing the Initial Woodland period. Although it is necessary for handling data and for communication to make such an arbitrary and artificial division, it unfortunately also creates the impression that the Initial Woodland period is somehow significantly different from the preceding Archaic period. This is not so! The Archaic populations continued their long established way of life with progressive changes taking place in the tools they used and in other aspects of their culture and burial practices. One new trait is added—pottery.

Indeed, the artificial nature of the separation of the late Archaic and early Woodland peoples can best be illustrated by considering a hypothetical village site occupied by Archaic people who do not possess pottery. Some time during their occupation the knowledge necessary to produce pottery vessels is introduced. As soon as these Archaic villagers begin to manufacture pottery they become, as a necessary convenience for the archæologists, Woodland peoples.

Pottery has been independently invented a number of times in both the New World and the Old. The knowledge of pottery that entered Ontario came from several completely independent sources. One of the first varieties of pottery to appear in Southern Ontario consists of simple beaker-shaped vessels. Cord impressions generally occur on both the exterior and the interior of these vessels, although some are carefully smoothed and others have the cord impressions on only the exterior or only the interior. Good evidence exists that the idea of pottery advanced northward from the southeastern United States where it had been known as early as 2000 B.C. Late Archaic peoples in southern and eastern New York, Pennsylvania, and Massachusetts had for many years manufactured cooking vessels out of easily carved soapstone. These people received the idea of pottery from further south and began producing pottery vessels identical to their earlier stone vessels. Somewhat later the beaker-shaped, cord-impressed and plain vessels were produced. It was the latter pottery variety that was adopted by late Laurentian Archaic peoples in New York state, the upper St. Lawrence

Valley region of Quebec, and the extreme eastern portions of Southern Ontario. These people have been described as Meadowood culture.

appears to have been a strong connection with the related mortuary practices of the mid-western United States. Graves are often profusely provided with grave goods manufactured from stone and copper and particularly large numbers of carefully flaked triangular flint blades that may have been specifically manufactured for placement with the dead. Archaic period tools such as gouges and spear-thrower weights have disappeared and new items such as the problematical birdstones, tubular pottery pipes, and ground slate gorgets appear for the first time. Natural minerals (hematite, limonite, and graphite), presumably used for painting the body and other objects, are a common occurrence in the graves. So is the abundant use of powdered hematite.

Meadowood culture (1000 B.C.-500 B.C.)

The Meadowood culture is known mainly from cemeteries excavated in adjacent New York state. The burial ceremonialism of the late Archaic period is continued and elaborated upon with cremation burial becoming quite common. There also

What little evidence we have from habitation sites in New York and Quebec suggests that the Meadowood people followed a life identical with that of their Archaic period ancestors. In Southern Ontario the Meadowood culture appears to have established itself only in the areas immediately adjacent to the province of Quebec and New York state. The reason for the limited occupation of Southern Ontario appears to be that the remaining Archaic peoples in the province adopted quite different pottery from that typical of the Meadowood culture. Certainly the Meadowood pottery, called Vinette 1, has been found throughout the rest of Southern Ontario but always in association with and dominated by pottery of a quite different variety. Similarly, the birdstones and ground slate gorgets are found throughout the rest of Southern Ontario and must have been adopted into the area from the same southern sources from which the Meadowood people received them.

The two major Initial Woodland populations that shared Southern Ontario with the Meadowood culture are called the Point Peninsula culture and the Saugeen culture.

Fig. 2. Initial Woodland period antler comb.

Point Peninsula culture
(700 B.C.-1000 A.D.)

It will be recalled that the Laurentian Archaic peoples of Southern Ontario were divided into eastern and western varieties, using the Toronto region as an approximate boundary. The Point Peninsula culture occupied roughly the same area as the eastern Laurentian group (southeastern Southern Ontario) as well as adjacent Quebec and New York. These peoples appear to have been the direct descendants of the earlier Archaic peoples.

A number of village sites as well as cemeteries of the Point Peninsula people have been investigated by archæologists. Most are small camp sites but a few cover many acres and must have been used seasonally for many years by successive generations of Point Peninsula peoples, as well as by earlier and later populations. The pottery used by the Point Peninsula culture came originally from three completely different sources. It was predominantly obtained from a pottery vessel complex characteristic of Manitoba, Northern Ontario and western Quebec. The origin of these northern ceramics is still somewhat of a problem. While they superficially resemble pottery vessels from Siberia, a gap of more than 2,000 miles separates the Asiatic sites from the most northwesterly sites in North America. Perhaps the similarities are not indicative of any historical connection; the ceramics in Northern Ontario may have evolved independently in the north. They certainly bear little similarity to the North American ceramics further south.

Another major pottery vessel complex that contributed to Point Peninsula culture came from the south, apparently originating in Central America and gradually spreading northward, receiving strong contributions from the even earlier pottery of the southeastern United States. This complex and gradual spread of pottery ideas from the south attained a high level of development in the Hopewell culture of Ohio and Illinois.

Hopewell culture, although having its roots in the earlier Archaic and Woodland cultures of the region, developed a relatively sophisticated society in which an elite priesthood presided over an elaborate religious cult. This cult included the construction of large burial mounds and other earth works. To meet the demands for the placement of exotic material with the bodies of privileged individuals buried in the mounds, the wide trade network, basically established during the Archaic period, was greatly expanded. This trade pattern involved copper from Lake Superior, marine shells from the Gulf of Mexico, obsidian from Wyoming, grizzly bear canine teeth from the western prairies, and a wide range of exotic flints and shark teeth from a variety of sources. In addition to the basically southern origin of Hopewell pottery and burial mounds, other traits such as clay human figurines, ear spools, and specialized flint flake knives appear to have come out of Central America along with revolutionizing religious beliefs. The development of Hopewell culture in the river valleys of Illinois and Ohio was to have a profound effect upon the Initial Woodland peoples of Southern Ontario. One of the earliest effects was the introduction of certain pottery vessel styles.

Thus, we are faced with the very complex situation whereby a late Laurentian Archaic population in southeastern Southern Ontario adopted ideas concerned with the manufacture of pottery vessels from both Northern Ontario and from the Hopewell area. A third source of pottery ideas, coming from the previously described Meadowood culture, also had an impact, although slight.

To add to all this complexity, the Archaic peoples of southeastern Southern Ontario, who were adopting their pottery from several completely different sources, obviously had their own ideas of what constituted a proper pottery vessel. They, therefore, appear to have taken all of these ideas coming from various sources and to have moulded them into something uniquely theirs.

If the intricacies by which the Archaic peoples of Southern Ontario finally came to adopt pottery seem to have been emphasized here, it is simply because pottery is a vital tool which enables the archæologist to trace subsequent prehistoric developments. Therefore it is necessary to understand clearly its varied origins. The methods used by the Point Peninsula people to decorate their pottery and their manner of shaping their vessels were quite different from the simple pottery of the Meadowood culture. Most commonly the Point Peninsula pottery vessels were decorated by

Plate 9. Point Peninsula culture artifacts.

Fig. a. Fragments from the rims of typical pottery vessels.

Fig. b. Ground slate pendant.

Fig. c. The notched soapstone pottery decorator to the right was used to produce the designs in the plasticene to the left.

Fig. d. Antler flaker painted with red ochre that would have been used for fashioning stone implements.

Fig. e. Bone awl.

Fig. f. Stone darts or arrowheads.

Fig. g. Two styles of soapstone pipes: the one on the left is the earliest.

Fig. h. Knife made from Pennsylvania jasper.

Fig. i. Polished stone adze.

Map 5. The Initial Woodland period trade networks.

impressing the wet clay with a series of notched or toothed implements that produced a wide range of distinctive and artistic designs. Although the ideas that eventually resulted in Point Peninsula pottery appear to have come from three distinct sources, it is apparent that the dominant influences came from the north.

At first the only significant difference between the Point Peninsula people and their Archaic ancestors was the possession of pottery and a few other minor traits. The basic way of life, developed during the Archaic period, had not changed nor had the burial ritual to any significant degree. The Point Peninsula people continued in their seasonal rounds to occupy the same sites as their ancestors. Natural internal changes, of course, occurred and we can see gradual modifications taking place in certain tools, the discontinuance of certain practices, and the adoption of some new ideas. On the whole, however, there are no major changes and one has the impression of small groups of hunters following the interminable rounds necessary for survival and not being overly interested in events outside their

immediate territory. At about the time of the birth of Christ outside ideas involved with burial practices begin to penetrate Point Peninsula culture. These ideas, associated with religion, came from the Hopewell culture of the Ohio area via New York state. The most dramatic feature of the new ideas adopted from the south was the construction of earth burial mounds.

Initially the southern practices appear to have simply been added to the indigenous Archaic-Meadowood burial pattern, but in a relatively short time the new and the old ideas fused to produce something unique. During this period stone implements, probably manufactured solely for placement with the dead, are frequently made from flint originating in Ohio, Pennsylvania, and eastern New York. The earlier Archaic period trading patterns, i.e. marine shells from both the Gulf of Mexico and the Atlantic and native copper from Lake Superior, are maintained. Items made from Ohio pipestone, Ontario silver (from Cobalt), and a distinctive Labrador quartzite appear in the graves. Ohio Valley items such as copper ear spools, stone platform pipes, worked wolf and bear skull parts (prob-

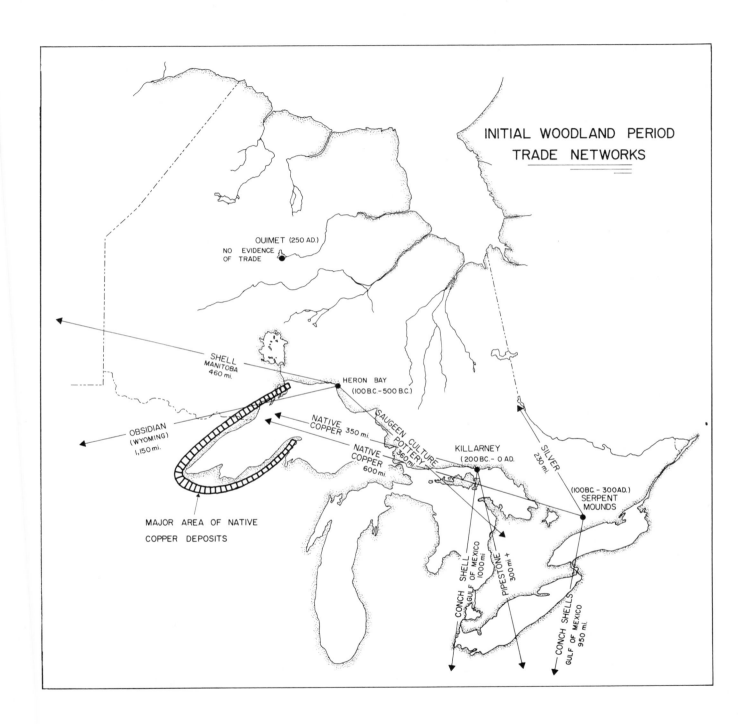

INITIAL WOODLAND PERIOD
TRADE NETWORKS

OUIMET (250 A.D.)
NO EVIDENCE
OF TRADE

SHELL
MANITOBA
460 mi.

HERON BAY
(100 B.C. – 500 B.C.)

OBSIDIAN
(WYOMING)
1,150 mi.

NATIVE
COPPER 350 mi.

SAUGEEN CULTURE
POTTERY
360 mi.

KILLARNEY
(200 B.C. – 0 A.D.)

SILVER
230 mi.

NATIVE
COPPER
600 mi.

(100 B.C. – 300 A.D.)
SERPENT
MOUNDS

MAJOR AREA OF NATIVE
COPPER DEPOSITS

CONCH SHELL
GULF OF MEXICO
1000 mi.

PIPESTONE
300 mi +

CONCH SHELLS
GULF OF MEXICO
950 mi.

Plate 10. The Donaldson site, a typical Saugeen culture village site, located beside a major rapid where sturgeon and drum could be speared. The small cemetery was located in the excavation to the far left. House structures, garbage dumps and pits were encountered in the excavations below the campsite. It is very likely that ancient houses also stood on the location of the tent camp. Serious erosion along the bank edge has already destroyed an unknown portion of the site.

ably portions of head-dresses) and copper pan-pipes also appear for the first time. Certainly the most impressive expression of the new burial practices is to be seen in the 194-foot-long "Serpent Mound" at Rice Lake, southeast of Peterborough. Southern Ontario sites directly involved in mound building and Hopewellian ceremonialism, however, are relatively few in number and are restricted to the St. Lawrence Valley and southern edges of the province.

Possibly such sites acted as ceremonial centres to which the people from the interior of the province made periodic visits. The majority of the stone and bone tools found in these sites, however, clearly reflect their Archaic antecedents. The study of the human skeletons suggests that these robust, round-headed people are derived from the same stock as the Archaic populations of the same general region. A detailed examination of the skeletons has revealed that they suffered from the same kinds of dental and physical ailments as their Archaic predecessors—ailments to be expected in a hunting population fully exposed to the hazards of their environment and the necessity of consuming coarse natural plant and animal foods. Arthritis was particularly common among adults of all ages and there have even been instances of tuberculosis (Pott's disease) recorded.

Although the information is limited, it appears that the new burial mound ceremonialism with its importation of exotic goods from widely separated areas of eastern North America began to decline by A.D. 400 and eventually disappeared. The reasons for this breakdown in the ritualistic treatment of the dead are unknown. One very likely reason, however, would be the declining ceremonialism of the Hopewell culture that had been the original stimulating force. Despite the disappearance of the elaborate burial rites, the basic way of life of the Point Peninsula people continued without significant change. Indeed, the unchanging seasonal food quest which began in the Palæo-Indian period was to be unbroken until the effective adaptation to agriculture during the Terminal Woodland period. Agriculture was introduced into Southern Ontario during the latter portion of the Initial Woodland period but it must have taken many years of gradual change to transform a hunting people into a farming people.

Saugeen culture
(700 B.C.- ?)

In most respects the Saugeen culture was very similar to the previously described Point Peninsula culture. Differences between the two populations appear to be the result of both their slightly different Laurentian Archaic ancestry and their different geographic locations. Although Saugeen pottery was adopted from the same varied sources as that of Point Peninsula culture, the former group developed their pottery styles in a somewhat different fashion. Burial mounds do not appear to have been constructed by the Saugeen people who buried their dead in small cemeteries. Other burial practices such as the lavishing of grave goods on infants and children rather than adults, the preference for flexed and bundle burials, and the depositing of red ochre, copper and marine shell implements and ornaments with the dead, are quite similar to those of the Point Peninsula peoples. Smoking pipes of any form, tubular or platform, appear to be absent.

The Saugeen village and camp sites that have been discovered to date are found along rapids or at the mouths of rivers and creeks emptying into Lake Huron and Lake Erie. Discarded food bones from these sites are predominantly fish, particularly large fish such as sturgeon and drum. Most types of fish found are spring to early summer river spawners, suggesting that the sites were occupied at the same time specifically to harvest the fish runs. These sites represent one segment of the seasonal rounds of the Saugeen people when the individual families gathered at a favourite fishing location during the spring to form a larger community. Perhaps marriages were contracted and various other ceremonies, involving the population as a whole, were carried out at this time. The villages may have been occupied throughout the summer and into the fall. Certainly for the first time substantial house structures can be recognized in the archæological

Fig. 3. Initial Woodland period stone platform pipe.

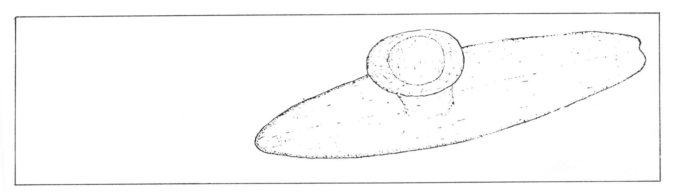

records. The houses, traced by the moulds left in the earth by the house wall and interior posts, were rectangular in shape, measured as much as 23 feet by 17 feet and contained hearths and pits. Apparently with the coming of winter these villages were abandoned and the individual families travelled to their winter hunting territories. Such a move was necessary for in the absence of stored foods such as corn, large numbers of people could not find sufficient food during the winter months and were forced to scatter across the country in small family groups.

For reasons that are unknown the coastal portion of Lake Huron that had been occupied so long by Archaic peoples and their Saugeen culture descendants was abandoned. Further to the south along the north shore of Lake Erie foreign influences coming from Michigan through the Windsor area and New York via the Niagara Peninsula replaced the earlier Saugeen culture. The intruding people and/or ideas are referred to as the Princess Point culture and appear to represent one of the late developments of the dramatically changing Hopewell culture.

a

b

c

d

e

f

g

h

i

j

Plate II. Saugeen culture artifacts.

Fig. a. Fragments from the rims of typical pottery vessels.

Fig. b. Dart heads: all these varieties are also typical of the preceding Archaic culture in the same general area.

Fig. c. Beaver incisor knife.

Fig. d. Polished slate gorget or pendant.

Fig. e. Native copper awl.

Fig. f. Native copper axe.

Fig. g. Polished stone adze.

Fig. h. Anvil stone that was also used as a hammerstone.

Fig. i. Elements from a necklace found around a young child's neck. The beads consist of native copper from the Lake Superior area and marginella shell beads from the Atlantic coast. Two ground bear canines were also strung on the necklace.

Fig. j. Scrapers.

Colour Plate IV. Iroquois effigy pipes.

The smoking pipes of the Iroquois-speaking peoples of northeastern North America represent an artistic achievement of exceptional standing. Produced in clay and more rarely in stone these pipes exhibit a significant degree of individuality while still conforming to certain accepted styles. Most of the pipe styles are restricted to specific regions that coincide with tribal groups although there is some overlap. Evidence now exists that certain pipe styles, particularly the effigy pipes, are probably associated with specific units of Iroquois society such as clans.

The effigy pipes illustrated on the opposite page were recovered from Ontario Iroquois and St. Lawrence Iroquois village sites, and all would date from approximately 1400 A.D. to the historic period. With the exception of four stone pipes, two in the upper right corner and two in the lower right corner, all pipes were modelled in clay. The range in animal subject matter is illustrated by the lower three pipes which, from left to right, represent a fish, a coiled snake, and an otter. As can be seen from the pipes in the centre of the picture, the owl was a favourite subject for the Iroquois artisan. It may also be noted that the human effigies range from highly stylized forms, such as the pipe at far right in the second row from the bottom, to quite life-like forms such as the pipe at far left in the same row.

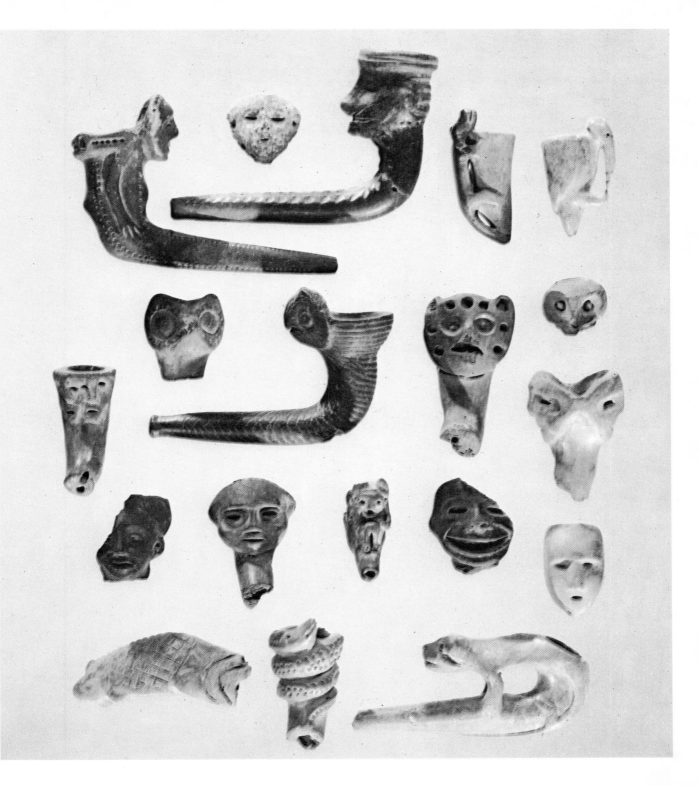

Princess Point culture
(500 A.D. - 1000 A.D.)

Very little is yet known of the Princess Point culture. Indeed, it has only recently been recognized as a distinct culture in the southwestern portions of Southern Ontario. The pottery complex of the Princess Point people bears no relationship to the earlier Saugeen culture pottery. It may have been introduced into Ontario via the Niagara Peninsula, the Windsor area or through both of these regions. This distinctive cord-malleated pottery, decorated for the most part with a cord-wrapped stick, shows its closest similarities with pottery styles found along the southern shores of Lake Erie. These styles very likely represent later ceramic developments out of the Hopewell culture.

At this early stage of investigation it is not known whether we are dealing with an actual migration of people into southwestern Southern Ontario or whether we are simply seeing the effect of southern pottery ideas being adopted and modified by local people. Whatever the case, there is a clear difference between the pottery complexes of the Princess Point culture and the preceding Saugeen culture.

It was probably through the Princess Point culture that corn agriculture was first introduced to Ontario.

While the Saugeen culture appears to have occupied nearly all of southwestern Southern Ontario, the Princess Point culture is only found close to the north shore of Lake Erie and the western end of Lake Ontario. Indeed, between 500 A.D. and 1000 A.D., the northern sections of southwestern Southern Ontario appear to have been abandoned. There are many things that are not known about the Initial Woodland period occupants of the regions to the north of Lake Erie. Who, for example, built the few burial mounds that have been discovered and for the most part, destroyed? Our knowledge of the Initial Woodland people of Northern Ontario is on a better footing.

Plate 12. Princess Point culture artifacts.

Fig. a. Fragments from the rims of typical pottery vessels.

Fig. b. Stone scraper.

Fig. c. Stone knives.

Fig. d. Stone drill.

Fig. e. Stone arrowhead.

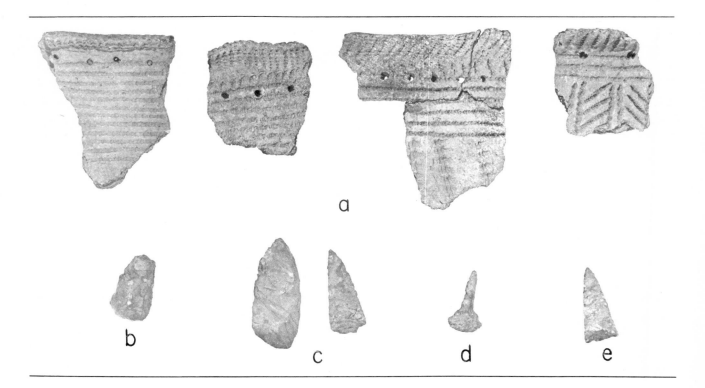

a

b

c

d

e

Laurel culture
(700 B.C. - 1000 A.D.)

Laurel culture sites have been found in east-central Saskatchewan, Manitoba, Northern Ontario, and in northwestern Quebec.

This widespread culture in the northern forests of the Canadian Shield basically represents the preceding Shield Archaic people with the addition of pottery. Where this pottery came from is still somewhat of a problem. It bears no apparent relationship to ceramics coming originally from Central America or the southeastern United States. At the same time it is separated by more than 2,000 miles from slightly similar pottery in Siberia. Perhaps it evolved independently in the northern forest of Canada after the idea of pottery was introduced from the south. Certainly Laurel pottery is related to the pottery of the Point Peninsula and Saugeen cultures of Southern Ontario, and it may have been from this region that the northerners obtained their knowledge of ceramics.

The Laurel peoples followed a way of life unchanged from that of their Archaic predecessors. One site, where the normally acid soil had been neutralized by the wood ash from ancient campfires, indicated that moose and beaver were the most important food animals. This site, however, was almost certainly a summer campsite and it can be expected that in other regions or at different seasons of the year other game animals or fish would have been more important. Indeed, in the more southerly territory of the Laurel people, wild rice gathering may well have been important.

Implements of chipped stone and bone have survived the rigours of time and many tools were made from the locally available native copper. Stone scraping tools for working hides, wood, and bone dominate the tool kit although arrowheads, lances, knives, hammerstones, and net-sinkers are common. Bone tools consist of awls, harpoons, beaver incisor knives, snowshoe netting needles and

Plate 13. Laurel culture burial mound on the banks of the Rainy River, with the state of Minnesota in the far background. The slice along the edge of the mound was done by a curious bulldozer operator. Mounds such as these may contain the remains of 100 or more individuals. The 6-foot-5-inch man beside the mound will give some idea of size.

pottery markers. The copper items are mainly beads, bangles, awls, parts of composite fishhooks, and chisels. Nothing, of course, survives of the wooden, bark, and leather goods that probably represented the most common and elaborate items of their material culture. Very common on most Laurel sites is red ochre in both nodule and powder form which would have been used as a pigment.

It is now apparent that these hunters of the harsh coniferous forests did not live in complete isolation from the outside world. The relationship of their ceramics to those of the Initial Woodland peoples of Southern Ontario has already been commented upon. They were almost certainly actively involved in trading native copper objects to people in the southeast. Such activities are never one way: Meadowood culture and Saugeen culture materials have been found on Laurel sites.

In the west, between Lake Superior and the Manitoba border, particularly along the Rainy River, numerous burial mounds were constructed by the Laurel people. These mounds are the largest prehistoric structures in all of Ontario and may contain up to 100 or more burials. Most of the mounds are over 50 feet in diameter and 6 feet in height although one mound attained a diameter of 113 feet and a height of 24 feet. Burials usually consist of a bundle of bone indicating that the body had been allowed to decompose on a scaffold or shallow grave prior to reburial in the mound. Grave goods are generally absent although the mounds are rich in broken pottery and tools as they were constructed by piling up basket loads of village debris. Burial mounds are restricted to the portions of Northern Ontario adjacent to Minnesota. There is little doubt that the mound ceremonialism was introduced to the Laurel people by the

Hopewell culture of southern Minnesota and their intermediaries. In one instance a typical Hopewell platform pipe was found in an Ontario mound. A number of Ontario sites have also produced tools made from obsidian, a volcanic glass, extensively traded into the Hopewell culture area from Yellowstone Park in Wyoming. Such Hopewell burial ceremonialism, however, appears to have expressed itself in only a very peripheral way as far as Laurel culture was concerned. Indeed, these mounds are only found in a very restricted portion of Northern Ontario and are totally absent from Manitoba and northwestern Quebec.

This brief description of Laurel culture ends our consideration of the Initial Woodland period. As will become readily apparent in the following examination of the Terminal Woodland period, however, the following cultures are in all likelihood the direct products of the Initial Woodland period cultures.

Plate 14. Laurel culture artifacts.

Fig. a. Fragments from the rims of typical pottery vessels.

Fig. b. Hammerstone.

Fig. c. Stone knife.

Fig. d. Beaver incisor knife.

Fig. e. Antler toggle-head harpoon. Such harpoons were very likely used for capturing large fish such as sturgeon.

Fig. f. Netsinker consisting of a natural flat rock notched at both ends.

Fig. g. Native copper arrowheads.

Fig. h. The various designs in the plasticene (left) were produced by means of the stone pottery decorator (right).

Fig. i. Copper chisel.

Fig. j. Copper needle.

Fig. k. Copper beads.

Fig. l. Stone arrowheads.

Fig. m. Scrapers.

Fig. n. Lance head.

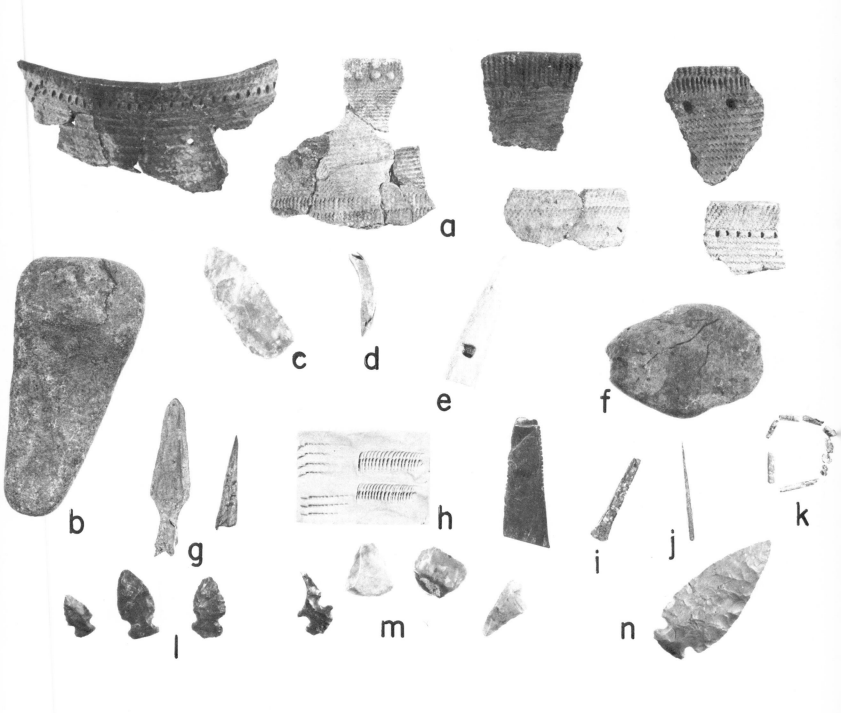

a　b　c　d　e　f

g　h　i　j　k

l　m　n

The Terminal Woodland Period (ca. 1000 A.D. to Historic Period)

Within the Terminal Woodland period of the province three cultural groupings will be considered. These are the Ontario Iroquois and the St. Lawrence Iroquois of Southern Ontario and the Algonkians (Ojibwa, Cree and Algonkins) of Northern Ontario. It should be pointed out that the term "Iroquois" is not limited to the famous Five Nations but has also been used to refer to closely related tribes such as the Huron, Petun, Neutral, Erie, and Susquehannock.

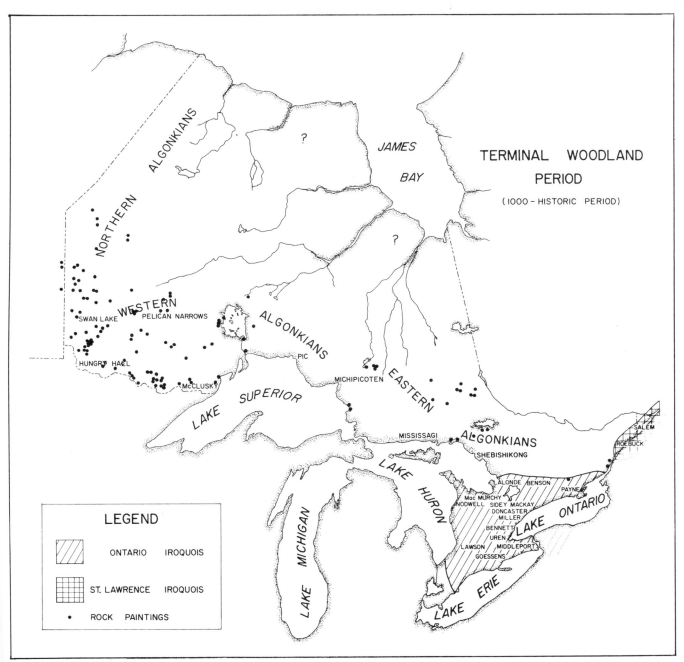

Map 6. The Terminal Woodland period.

The Ontario Iroquois

The prehistoric events which led to the historic Huron, Petun, Neutral, and Erie can be traced with a high degree of certainty to approximately 900 A.D. The point has already been reached where the Initial Woodland period ancestors of the Ontario Iroquois are being recognized. Our understanding of the culture of the Ontario Iroquois has been tremendously increased by the writings of missionaries and explorers who lived among these people during the first half of the seventeenth century. The major historical sources are the Jesuit *Relations* and the journals of Samuel de Champlain and Gabriel Sagard. Much of the information recovered by ethnologists working with living Five Nations Iroquois has also been extremely valuable in achieving a more accurate reconstruction of the prehistoric culture under consideration.

There is no question that the archæological, historical, and ethnological information available for the Ontario Iroquois exceeds that of any other archæological culture in Ontario and that the direct historical approach can be applied with greatest effectiveness. This does not mean that there are not gaps in our knowledge or areas of controversy—quite the contrary. It does mean, however, that of all the archæologically recognized populations of the province, we can speak with the greatest authority on the Ontario Iroquois and particularly on the Huron.

The recognized culture history of the Ontario Iroquois begins in the tenth century. At this time two populations possessing the essentials of Iroquois culture were developing in Southern Ontario. Tribal designations are not completely applicable at this early period. The population in southeastern Southern Ontario is called Pickering, and the population in southwestern Southern Ontario is known as Glen Meyer. Both of these names are taken from small present-day villages where the pertinent archæological remains were first discovered. It is a common practice of archæologists to name prehistoric cultural groups after landowners, towns, or some other current term when it is not possible to associate the archæological remains directly with an historically identified native population.

From 900 A.D. to 1300 A.D. these two groups of contemporaneous peoples (Pickering and Glen Meyer) developed in a parallel fashion and the archæological trends progressively approach the cultural pattern of the historic Iroquois.

The essential elements of Iroquois culture recognizable by archæological means consist of the following: a) corn agriculture supplemented by fishing and hunting; b) large villages up to 10 acres in extent, frequently palisaded and located in easily defensible positions removed from navigable water routes; c) the construction of longhouses; d) a pipe smoking complex; e) bundle burials (the disarticulated skeleton of an individual who was first placed on a scaffold or in a shallow grave prior to reburial as a bone bundle), including small ossuaries (pits containing a number of bundle burials) in and around the village—although the Pickering people also practised flexed burials; f) the use of the dog as a food animal and possibly for sacrifice; g) an archæological material culture dominated by pottery of essentially Iroquois character; and h) stone and bone tools which persist in later Iroquois culture.

Archæologically the Pickering and Glen Meyer cultures are quite similar. There are, however, some distinct differences between these groups which are the result of the different Initial Woodland period ancestry.

With reference to the Pickering people, for example, there is good evidence that their earliest pottery styles evolved out of Point Peninsula culture. A detailed examination of skeletal materials has also led the physical anthropologists to suggest that basically the same local racial stock of the Archaic period carried through the Initial Woodland period to the Pickering culture and later Iroquois peoples.

The pottery of the Glen Meyer people, on the other hand, appears to have stemmed from the Princess Point culture of the Initial Woodland period along with certain other traits. Unfortunately there is insufficient skeletal information to trace the racial relations such as was possible with the Pickering culture. While many of the basic cultural elements and, indeed, the basic way of life, of the Pickering and

Plate 15. Glen Meyer culture artifacts.

Fig. a. Fragments from the rims of typical pottery vessels.

Fig. b. Polished stone adze used for woodworking.

Fig. c. Slate pebble modified into pendant by drilling a suspension hole.

Fig. d. Typical small, crude pottery pipe.

Fig. e. Bone awl, presumably used in the production of skin clothing.

Fig. f. Stone scraper.

Fig. g. Stone arrowheads.

Fig. h. Bead made from native copper.

Fig. i. Stone drill.

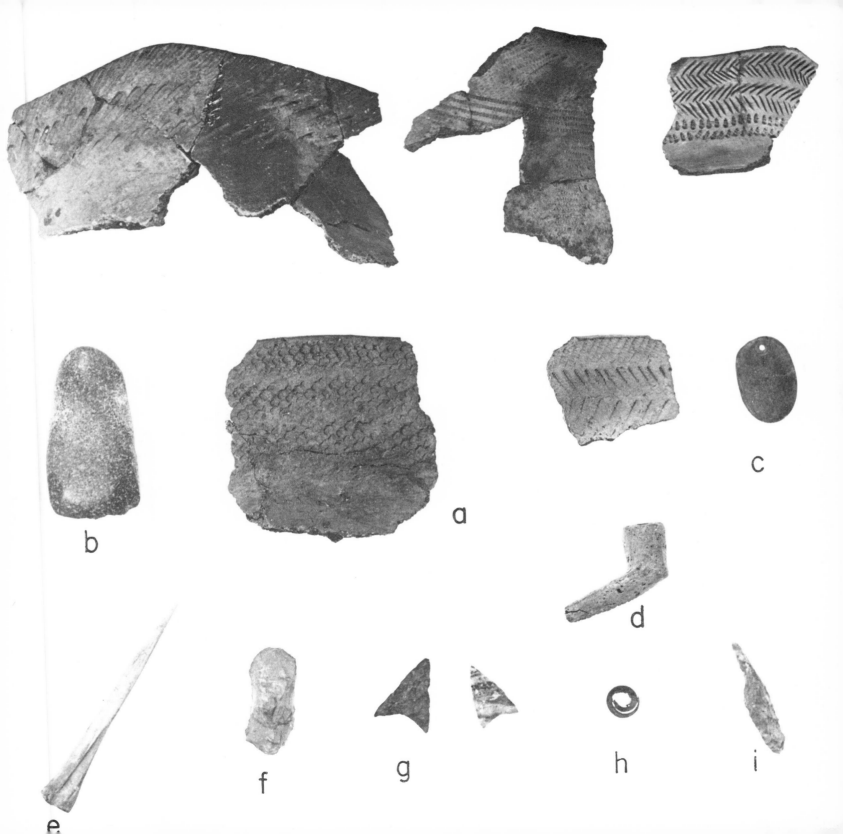

b

a

c

d

e

f

g

h

i

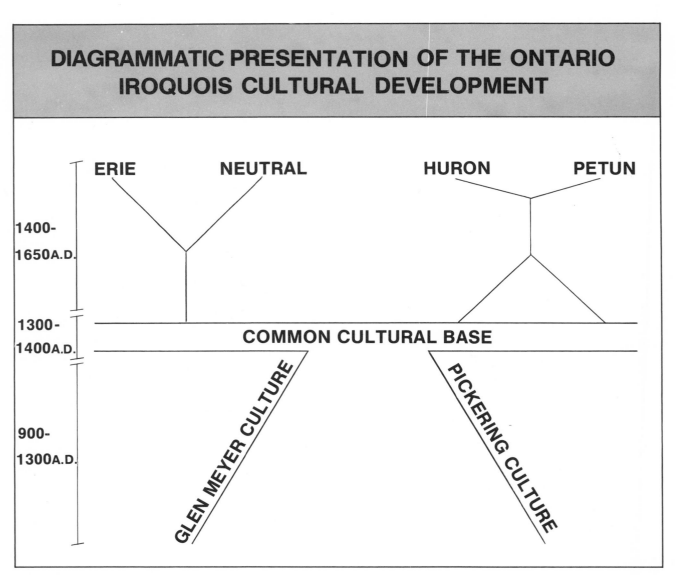

Diagram 4. Ontario Iroquois cultural development.

Glen Meyer peoples are quite similar their different Initial Woodland period ancestry allows the archæologist to clearly differentiate between the two groups.

Future research holds great promise for establishing a much clearer understanding of the cultural transition between the Initial and Terminal Woodland periods and, therefore, it can be anticipated that the beginnings of the Terminal Woodland period will be pushed well beyond the artificial and somewhat arbitrary 1000 A.D. dividing line. The artificiality of this convenient time marker of 1000 A.D. should already be apparent in the fact that 900 A.D. is the recognized beginning of both the Pickering and Glen Meyer cultures. In the future we hope to be able to discard such cumbersome handling of the time column but at this early stage in our understanding of Ontario prehistory it is still a useful device. Certainly in terms of the Ontario Iroquois, the period when the people became part-time farmers of corn, as well as hunters, would represent a more logical point of differentiation between the Initial and Terminal Woodland periods. At our present stage of knowledge corn agricul-

ture could have been introduced via either the late Point Peninsula or Princess Point cultures and most likely the latter. Corn and beans were originally domesticated in Mexico. But it took many thousands of years for agriculture to spread since time was required for new strains of plants to adapt to the shorter growing season and harsher climate of the north.

To summarize, the archæological information suggests that between 900 A.D. and 1300 A.D. Southern Ontario was occupied by two related populations practising corn agriculture supplemented by hunting and fishing. A chronic warfare pattern is indicated by the palisaded villages located on easily defended hillocks flanked by stream-cut ravines. The presence of longhouses indicates that a number of different families lived in each dwelling—in contrast to the earlier, small one-family houses. These early longhouses were smaller than the Iroquois longhouses of the historic period, but were otherwise similar. The clustering of such longhouses in palisaded villages suggests the possible existence of the independent or semi-independent village dominated by a single clan as recorded

Plate 16. Pickering culture artifacts.

Fig. a. Fragments from the rims of typical pottery vessels.

Fig. b. Bone awl.

Fig. c. Pottery gaming disc.

Fig. d. Typical small, simple pottery pipes.

Fig. e. Scraper.

Fig. f. Polished stone adze used in woodworking.

Fig. g. Anvil stone which also functioned as a hammerstone.

Fig. h. Arrowheads.

Fig. i. Deer toe bone, modified in a fashion typical of this culture but for an unknown purpose.

in the historic records. Bundle burials scattered in and around the villages appear to represent the beginnings of the ossuary burial pattern. Indeed, an ossuary containing 11 individuals is reported for the beginning of the twelfth century. Archæological evidence of widespread trade relations is extremely limited, suggesting that the populations developed in relative isolation.

At approximately 1300 A.D. a portion of the Pickering population expanded to the southwest and conquered the Glen Meyer people. Recent evidence suggests further that a somewhat earlier expansion by the Pickering culture had taken place to the northeast down the St. Lawrence River, in part laying the cultural base for the development of the St. Lawrence Iroquois. The dispersal and partial absorption of the Glen Meyer people by the Pickering people created a relatively uniform cultural occupation across most of Southern Ontario and the adjacent portion of southwestern New York. This uniform occupation was actually the product of two processes: the continuing development of the Pickering culture in southeastern Southern Ontario, and the conquest of southwestern Southern Ontario

by the Pickering people with the consequent partial absorption and dispersal of the Glen Meyer population. The conquerors of southwestern Southern Ontario and New York state, however, adopted a number of the characteristics of the conquered people. This suggests that the Iroquois pattern of mass adoption of enemy women and children to recoup war losses was already in existence. Substantial numbers of Glen Meyer people, however, apparently escaped by fleeing to southeastern Michigan and adjacent Ohio where Glen Meyer sites suddenly appear around 1300 A.D.

The influx of Glen Meyer traits into the culture of the Pickering invaders offers an explanation for the historic cultural and dialect differences between the Huron-Petun and the Neutral-Erie. If the conquest outlined above is accurate, then the Huron-Petun are the product of an unbroken Pickering cultural development in southeastern Southern Ontario. The Neutral-Erie, on the other hand, stemmed from the regional development of isolated Pickering colonists influenced by absorbed cultural elements from the earlier Glen Meyer population. Further, the very fact that a military conquest of this magnitude could have taken place must have meant that the Pickering people were capable of organizing a number of their villages into a confederacy for purposes of large-scale military operations.

For approximately 100 years between 1300 A.D. and 1400 A.D. a relatively homogeneous culture covered Southern Ontario and adjacent southwestern New York. During this period a number of significant elements were adopted or elaborated by the Ontario Iroquois. Sunflower seeds, used mainly for their oil, appear in the garbage dumps for the first time—as do charred and fragmented human remains which tentatively suggest the beginnings of cannibalism. Large ossuary burials, containing the remains of hundreds of people are present. By approximately 1350 A.D. an elaborate pipe complex is adopted from contemporaneous populations in the east who are eventually to become the historic Mohawk-Onondaga-Oneida. With this introduction of a highly developed pipe complex, smoking of tobacco for the first time becomes a common habit.

By 1400 the four historic tribes constituting the Ontario Iroquois begin to evolve out of their common cultural base. The Neutral develop in southwestern Southern Ontario, and the Erie in southwestern New York. In southeastern Southern Ontario two closely related populations occupy different geographic regions. One group evolved in Huronia proper between Lake Simcoe and Georgian Bay, while to the south, the other group developed in the valleys of rivers which empty into the north shore of Lake Ontario. Archæological evidence indicates that the southern group gradually advanced up the rivers towards Huronia and that the merging of the two closely related populations laid the basis for the Huron and the Petun of the historic period.

During the period when the four tribes separated from their common cultural base (1400 A.D.), beans and squash appear for the first time. With the combination of corn and beans, a nutritionally self-sufficient agricultural base was realized which markedly reduced the necessity of relying upon game to supplement the corn diet. There certainly ap-

Plate 17. Ontario Iroquois culture artifacts (typical of the period 1300 A.D.- 1400 A.D.).

Fig. a. Fragments from the rims of typical vessels.

Fig. b. Pipe on the upper left is characteristic of the sophisticated clay pipes introduced into Ontario from a cultural development in New York state that would eventually give rise to the Mohawk-Onondaga-Oneida.

Pipe on the upper right is characteristic of the crude and simple clay pipes of the preceding Glen Meyer and Pickering cultures.

Specimen to the right is a simple stone pipe.

Clay pipe stem to the left has been fashioned in the form of a corn cob.

Lower specimen is a pottery pipe which still retains the black paint stripes across the back of the lizard.

Fig. c. A worked deer toe bone that may have been attached to clothing as an ornament.

Fig. d. Bone comb or hair piece with only one tooth surviving.

Fig. e. Two bone awls.

Fig. f. Bone netting needle.

Fig. g. Bone flute or whistle.

Fig. h. Antler tool for flaking stone.

Fig. i. Small stone adze for wood-working.

Fig. j. Perforated pottery gaming disc.

Fig. k. Stone arrowheads.

Fig. l. Juvenile pottery vessel.

Fig. m. Perforated bear canine which was possibly part of a necklace.

Fig. n. Stone scraper.

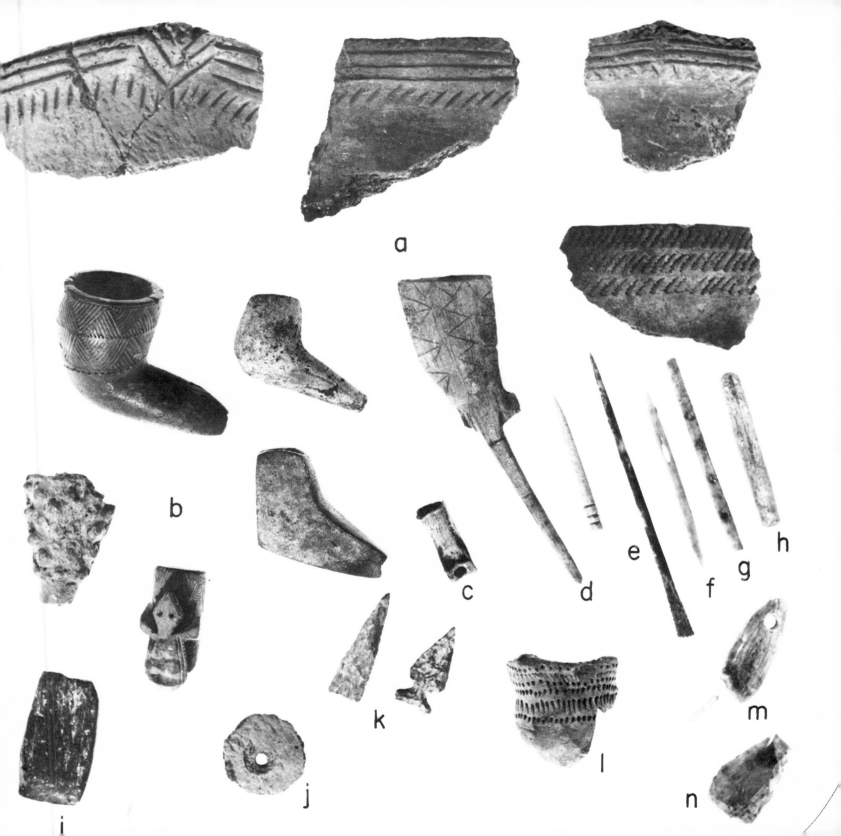

a

b

c

d

e

f

g

h

i

j

k

l

m

n

Plate 18. Late Pickering culture burial (1250 A.D.) of a young man who was a hunchback as a result of Pott's disease (spinal tuberculosis).

Plate 19. Model of Huron village based upon archæological and historical information.

Plate 20. Cut-away model of Huron longhouse showing interior details such as strung together corn suspended from the ceiling, sleeping platforms, and the central hearths. The human figures provide an approximation of scale.

pears to be a relationship between the addition of beans to the diet and the sharp population increase, reflected in the increasing size and number of villages and ossuaries. Cannibalism also shows a marked increase and appears to reach its peak around 1500 A.D.

The first direct contact of the Ontario Iroquois with Europeans came in 1615 A.D. when the Récollets and then later (1625 A.D.) the Jesuits began missionary activities among the Huron and, to a lesser degree, the Petun. Also Samuel de Champlain became actively involved in the wars of the Algonkians and the various Iroquois tribes. A close relationship between the French and the Huron-Petun was maintained until 1649 A.D. The involvement of the Ontario Iroquois in the fur trade and the political intrigues of European powers, however, was to prove disastrous. As a result the culture history of these people terminates with their dispersal and absorption by the Iroquois League of Five Nations (Mohawk, Onondaga, Oneida, Seneca, and Cayuga) between 1649 and 1654 A.D.

Plate 21. Huron-Petun Iroquois culture artifacts.

Fig. a. Fragments from the rims of typical pottery vessels.

Fig. b. Juvenile vessel made by a small girl learning the potter's art.

Fig. c. Stone pipe to which a wooden stem would have been attached. Notice the small hole at the base of the pipe: the bowl was attached to the stem by a string and could not accidentally be broken or lost if it became detached from the stem.

Fig. d. Antler harpoon.

Fig. e. Scraper.

Fig. f. Netting needle, presumably used in the production of nets and other loosely woven items.

Fig. g. Stone turtle amulet.

Fig. h. Stone and bone arrowheads.

Fig. i. Typical clay smoking pipes.

Fig. j. Bone dagger made from one of the human forearm (ulna) bones.

a

b

c

d

e

f

g

h

i

j

Fig. 4. Archæological floor plan from a 1550 A.D. St Lawrence Iroquois village site 50 miles south of Ottawa. The floor plan of one house, 123 feet long, is completely exposed. The excavations have also revealed part of the floor plans of two other houses. Sections of the defences are to be seen in the lower left-hand corner. At least three lines of palisade posts are involved with the innermost line apparently being torn down to make room for additional houses as the village expanded.

The black dots represent post moulds left by posts; the circular and ovate outlines represent pits; and the central features filled with diagonal lines are hearths.

If two families shared a single central hearth, as was the case during the historic period, then as many as 50 people (10 families) could have lived in the house at the bottom of this village plan.

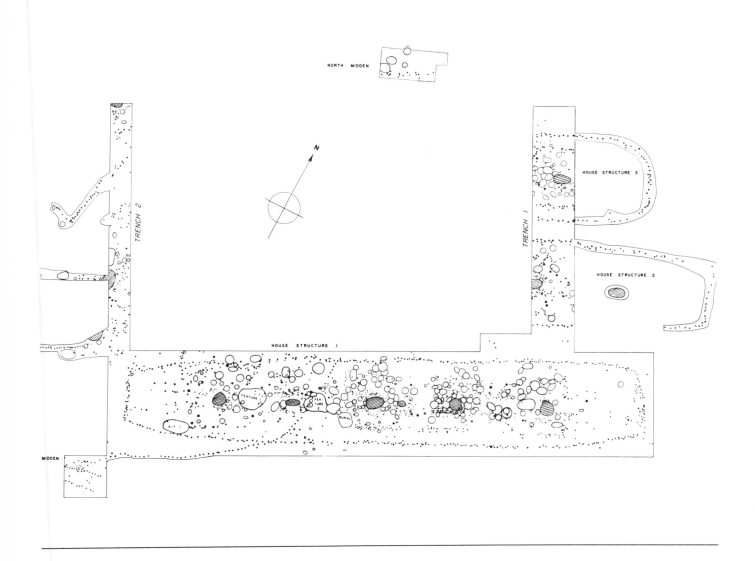

Plate 22. Neutral-Erie Iroquois culture artifacts.

Fig. a. Fragments from the rims of typical pottery vessels.

Fig. b. Gorget or pendant made from a human skull cap.

Fig. c. Stone and bone arrowheads.

Fig. d. Antler comb or, more likely, a hair piece.

Fig. e. Wooden spoon.

Fig. f. Beaver incisor knife.

Fig. g. Antler flaker used for chipping flint into finished tools.

Fig. h. Antler chisel.

Fig. i. Natural slate pebble drilled to form a pendant.

Fig. j. Elaborately decorated bone awl.

Fig. k. Box turtle modified into a rattle.

Fig. l. Typical clay smoking pipes.

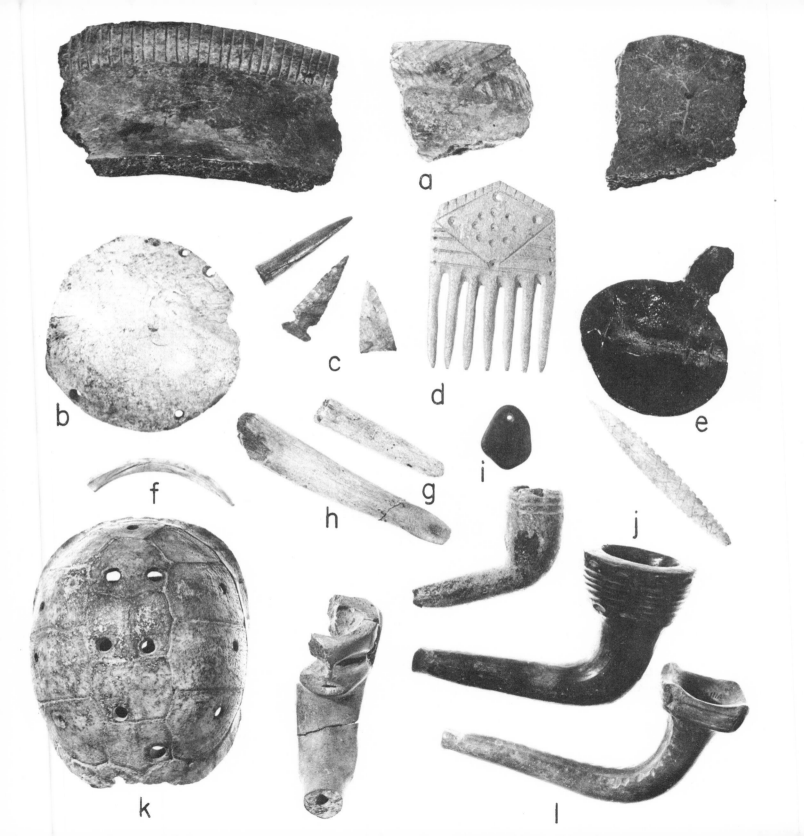

a

b

c

d

e

f

g

h

i

j

k

l

The St. Lawrence Iroquois

In 1535 A.D. Jacques Cartier visited the village of Hochelaga on the present site of the city of Montreal. In 1603 A.D. Samuel de Champlain found that the village of Hochelaga and related villages along the upper St. Lawrence River were abandoned. Who were these people and what had happened to them between 1535 A.D. and 1603 A.D.?

Until recently a number of archæologists believed that the people encountered by Cartier were the Onondaga who had been driven from the St. Lawrence Valley by their Algonkian enemies and were forced to take up residence in their historic homeland in New York state. Recent research in New York, however, has revealed that the Onondaga are very closely related to the nearby Mohawk and Oneida and that they have always lived in their approximate historic location. It is now apparent that the St. Lawrence Iroquois were an independent group of Iroquois people who were destroyed some time between the visits of Cartier and Champlain.

Village sites of the St. Lawrence Iroquois occur along the upper St. Lawrence Valley in southern Quebec, eastern Ontario, and adjacent New York state. Some impression of the size and appearance of these villages can be obtained from Jacques Cartier's description of Hochelaga.

The village is circular and is completely enclosed by a wooden palisade in three tiers like a pyramid. The top one is built crosswise, the middle one perpendicular and the lowest one of strips of wood placed lengthwise. The whole is well joined and lashed after their manner, and is some two lances in height. There is only one gate and entrance to this village, and that can be barred up. Over this gate and in many places about the enclosure are species of galleries with ladders for mounting to them, which galleries are provided with rocks and stones for the defence and protection of the place. There are some fifty houses in this village, each about fifty or more paces in length and twelve or fifteen in width, built completely of wood and covered in and bordered up with large pieces of the bark and rind of trees, as broad as a table, which are well and cunningly lashed after their manner. And inside these houses are many rooms and chambers; and in the middle is a large space without a floor, where they light their fire and live together in common. Afterwards the men retire to the above mentioned quarters with their wives and children. And furthermore there are lofts in the upper part of their houses, where they store the corn of which they make their bread.

If Cartier's estimate of the number of houses and their dimensions is accurate, then there could well have been more than 2,000 people living in this single St. Lawrence Iroquois village. That his estimates were within reason is suggested by recent excavations on a St. Lawrence Iroquois site in eastern Ontario. The dimensions of eight longhouses were determined at this site and they ranged from 60 feet to 135 feet in length with an average of more than 96 feet. An estimate of the total number of longhouses at the site is 40.

Most of what has already been said for the Ontario Iroquois applies equally well to the St. Lawrence Iroquois. This is, per-haps, not too surprising when it is realized that a northeastern expansion of the Pickering culture appears to have laid the cultural base for the eventual development of the St. Lawrence Iroquois. In other words, some time prior to 1300 A.D. the same culture that was eventually to give rise to the Huron, Petun, Neutral, and Erie to the west also was the cultural foundation from which the St. Lawrence Iroquois would evolve. Although possessing a culture basically similar to their western kinsmen, the St. Lawrence Iroquois were to develop in a locally distinctive fashion. For example, rather than practising ossuary burial they buried their dead in flexed positions throughout the village. Their methods of decorating pottery and pipes were distinctively different and they made far greater use of bone for fashioning tools. Cannibalism was far more common than among even the Huron. The garbage dumps contain abundant evidence of charred and broken human bones as well as ornaments and tools made from parts of the human skeleton. When it is possible to identify the sex and age of these human bones they are found to be parts of adult males. This agrees with the evidence of historic

Plate 23. St. Lawrence Iroquois culture artifacts.

Fig. a. Fragments from the rims of typical pottery vessels.

Fig. b. Bone and stone arrowheads.

Fig. c. Soapstone beads.

Fig. d. Distinctive pottery pipe form whose symbolic meaning is unknown.

Fig. e. Typical pottery smoking pipes. The uppermost specimen was probably made by a young boy who had not yet mastered the art of pipe manufacture.

Fig. f. Gaming disc made from a decorated fragment of pottery.

Fig. g. To the left, a gorget or pendant made from a human skull cap—such items were very likely war trophies.

Above, a ground deer toe bone—such objects are very common in most late Iroquois sites but their function is unknown.

Fig. h. This rare specimen is a human figurine produced in pottery.

Fig. i. Bone fish-hook.

Fig. j. Deer shoulder blade that has been modified in a clever fashion into a smoking pipe.

Fig. k. Juvenile pottery vessel.

a

b

c

d

e

f

g

h

i

j

k

records that the Iroquois tortured and ate adult males but adopted the women and children not killed in the heat of battle.

Although we are not completely certain of what happened to the St. Lawrence Iroquois, some suggestive evidence has appeared on the mid-sixteenth-century Huron sites along the Trent waterway. All of these Huron sites possess a high percentage of the distinctive St. Lawrence Iroquois pottery. Such pottery is even found as far west as Huron sites in the Toronto area. It may be speculated that the Hurons on the Trent River system and possibly their kinsmen in the Toronto region waged a successful war against the St. Lawrence Iroquois to the east. We have already seen that at a much earlier period the Ontario Iroquois were capable of forming military confederacies for purposes of carrying out major conquests of adjacent populations, e.g. Pickering culture dispersal and absorption of the Glen Meyer culture. If such a conquest took place, it can be expected that many of the conquered women and children would be carried back to the villages of the victors, eventually to be adopted fully into the new community. At the same time, these female captives would continue to make their traditional pottery and therein may well lie the explanation for the strong and relatively sudden influx of St. Lawrence Iroquois pottery styles in the Huron sites to the west. Conversely, the characteristic smoking pipes of the St. Lawrence Iroquois do not occur on these Huron sites. If, as there are some reasons to believe, smoking pipes were made by men rather than women, then their absence would reinforce the proposal that St. Lawrence Iroquois culture came to a violent end at the hands of the Hurons.

It would be very convenient if we could refer to the northern Algonkian-speakers who occupied Ontario as Algonkins, Ojibwa, and Cree. These names, however, are actually somewhat artificial terms used in referring to groupings of many small, independent bands of hunters who were loosely related through marriage and clan affiliations and, more generally, through language and way of life. Tribal designations equivalent to those used in describing the Iroquois-speaking people of Southern Ontario cannot be applied to the Algonkian-speakers of Northern Ontario.

An examination of a 1680 A.D. French map, which locates the native people of Ontario, gives some idea of the problem. Running from east to west we have the Algonquins and Petite Nation along the north side of the Ottawa River; the Nipissiens, Sorciers, and Missisaghe in the Lake Nipissing region; the Sauteurs at Sault Ste. Marie; the Gens du Nord, Kilistinons, and Bagouache north of Lake Superior and east of Lake Nipigon; the Alamepigons at Lake Nipigon; and the Outaouacs to the west of Lake Nipigon. How does one divide up these names into Algonkin, Ojibwa, or Cree? The Kilistinons, for example, are generally taken to be the Cree but if so, what is their relationship in 1680 A.D. to the Bagouache to the south, the Alamepigons to the northwest, and the Gens du Nord to the northeast. And in 1680 A.D. did the term Kilistinons always refer to the Cree?

The problem is that we are dealing with small, independent bands of people who were closely related in terms of both language and culture and who were described by early Europeans under a host of different names. Some of these names appear to refer to clans, bands, chiefs, and geographical locations and frequently a number of different names were used for the same population. On other occasions a single name was given a very wide application. For example, the name Ottawa (equated with Outaouacs) has been referred to as "a term common to the Cree, Algonkin, Nipissing, Montagnais, Ottawa, and Chippewa."

The impossible task of assigning tribal names to the Terminal Woodland peoples of Northern Ontario has been avoided by describing them all under the language designation "Algonkian." As both arch-æological research and studies of the historic documents progress, it may some day be possible to arrive at finer distinctions. At this time it is probably of more use to discuss these people, whose most significant social unit was the individual family, under the broadest of designations.

Archæological knowledge of the Algonkians of Northern Ontario is both recent and limited. These weaknesses, however, are partly compensated for by the existence of stratified sites containing the accumulated debris of seasonal occupations spanning a number of centuries. A stratified site is something like a layer-cake with the bottom layer being the earliest and the top layer the latest. On the basis of a very few sites, therefore, it is possible to examine the culture history of the Algonkians from the historic period to approximately the tenth century.

In applying the direct historical approach to the Algonkian, we frequently find a contrast with the application of the method to the Ontario Iroquois. For example, ceramics are relied upon heav-ily to trace the culture history of the Ontario Iroquois as the archæological evidence suggests that tribe and dialect roughly correlate with ceramic style in Iroquois culture. Conversely, the evidence from Algonkian archæology indicates that frequently ceramics were a borrowed element or, more accurately, an erratically introduced element which was not strongly integrated in the native culture. Among the eastern and southern Algonkian bands of Northern Ontario, in particular, two or more different ceramic traditions frequently appear together. The frequency or even presence of these completely different ceramic traditions will vary through time at a single stratified site. Also, contemporaneous Algonkian sites only a short distance from each other will possess different ceramic traditions. Pottery styles are certainly of value in tracing the various directions from which influences were received by the Algonkian bands and also serve as useful time markers. They are, however, not sufficiently consistent in certain areas to allow the archæologist to establish dependable cultural sequences. The stone tools, on the other hand, do not appear to be as subject to inconsistencies as the ceramics and can be used to arrive at consistent relationships through both time and space.

An explanation for this situation, which is so different from the Iroquois, may be found in Algonkian social structure. In these northern areas where food was scarce it would have been necessary for the hunters to be intimately familiar with the habits and densities of the local animals that could be used for food. A hunter would also require the assistance of close kinsmen such as brothers and uncles. The scanty food supply also severely limited the number of people who could survive in an area and, therefore, the human population densities were quite low. Under conditions of sparse population it becomes increasingly difficult for men to obtain marriageable women due to close blood or clan relations and, therefore, women had to be obtained from outside areas.

The woman's basic functions of rearing the children, tending the fish nets, and carrying out general camp duties meant that she could move great distances and still function as an effective person in the community. The man, on the other hand, had to possess a detailed knowledge of the local animal resources and required the assistance of close kinsmen in exploiting these resources. Women were simply far more mobile than men. As pottery manufacturing is a trait of female culture, the mixture of different ceramic traditions at single sites may be a reflection of female mobility in response to the necessary local residence of the males. Conversely, the relative stability seen in the varieties of stone tools may be a natural expression of the local male culture.

To illustrate more clearly this complex state of affairs, we could postulate a situation where three brothers living on a site along the north shore of Lake Superior required wives at the same time but there were no marriageable women in their small, local community. If one brother obtained a wife from Lake Nipissing, another from northern Wisconsin, and the remaining brother from the west end of Lake Superior, their three hypothetical Algonkian-speaking wives would eventually be sitting together at the same site making completely different types of pottery vessels. This pattern of quite often obtaining one's wife from a distant area still exists. The cultural and linguistic homogeneity of the northern Algonkians that today still permits natives of northern Saskatchewan to converse with natives in Labrador must have been, at least in part, maintained by this female mobility.

Massive forest fires that occasionally destroyed thousands of square miles of forest must also have forced various bands of these northern hunters to shift from one location to another in a somewhat erratic fashion and thereby assist the homogenizing effect upon the language and the culture. The loose, highly individualistic social structure, whereby families and individuals could leave one band or leader to join another, would also have been an important factor.

Despite this apparent cultural fluidity, there is sufficient archæological evidence to propose three major areas of Algonkian development in Northern Ontario. These areas may be roughly categorized as eastern, western, and northern.

the eastern area

The Eastern area of Algonkian cultural development extends northward to Lake Abitibi, westward to the northeast shore of Lake Superior, and on the east is adjacent to the Huron and Petun cultural development

Pottery styles in this area are predominantly derived from the Huron-Petun ceramic development. Those eastern Algonkians closest to the Ontario Iroquois area were directly involved in the same ceramic tradition as their Iroquois neighbours from approximately 900 A.D. to the historic period. Around the east end of Lake Superior, Huron-Petun pottery styles did not become prevalent until 1450 A.D. Earlier ceramic traditions coming from northern Michigan and Wisconsin are more characteristic of the earlier pottery styles and persist to the historic period along with the Huron-Petun ceramics. Other cultural elements adopted by the eastern Algonkians from the Huron-Petun are smoking pipes and, to an unknown degree, ossuary burial. Ignoring the pottery and pipes for a moment, however, the stone and bone tools of the eastern Algonkian were distinctively different as were their houses. Dog burials are also far more common than among the adjacent Huron-Petun where dog remains most commonly appear in the garbage dumps as discards from a feast. Certain of the eastern Algonkian bands had also adopted corn agriculture from their Iroquois neighbours but in a half-hearted fashion. The crop was planted in the spring, abandoned during the summer and the remnant left by the racoons, birds, and insects was harvested in the fall.

The apparently close relationship between the eastern Algonkians and the Huron-Petun is further substantiated by the historic documents. When the first French missionaries and explorers arrived in Huronia a flourishing trade already existed between the Huron and the eastern Algonkians. This trade basically involved the Hurons trading corn and fish-nets for furs and meat. It also appears that in these trading ventures it was the Algonkians who learned to speak Huron rather than the reverse. The Hurons, on the other hand, obtained the birchbark canoe from the Algonkians and adopted their style of house during their fishing expeditions to the islands of Georgian Bay. While there is some evidence of reciprocity in the dealings between the eastern Algonkians and the Hurons, it is apparent that the latter were the dominant partners.

It is perhaps not too surprising that the strong Iroquois influences seen on the eastern Algonkian sites reflect similar influences coming into the area from Southern Ontario during the Initial Woodland period and even the preceding Archaic period. The populations of this area appear to have always been subjected to strong cultural forces originating from Southern Ontario.

Plate 24. Eastern Algonkian artifacts.

Fig. a. Fragments from the rims of pottery vessels typical of two completely independent pottery traditions—one from Southern Ontario (two central specimens) and the other from western Michigan and eastern Wisconsin.

Fig. b. Large slate scraper.

Fig. c. Two clay pipes copied or obtained by trade from the Hurons or the Petuns.

Fig. d. Native copper finger ring.

Fig. e. Native copper awl.

Fig. f. Crude stone chisel.

Fig. g. Scrapers

Fig. h. Arrowheads.

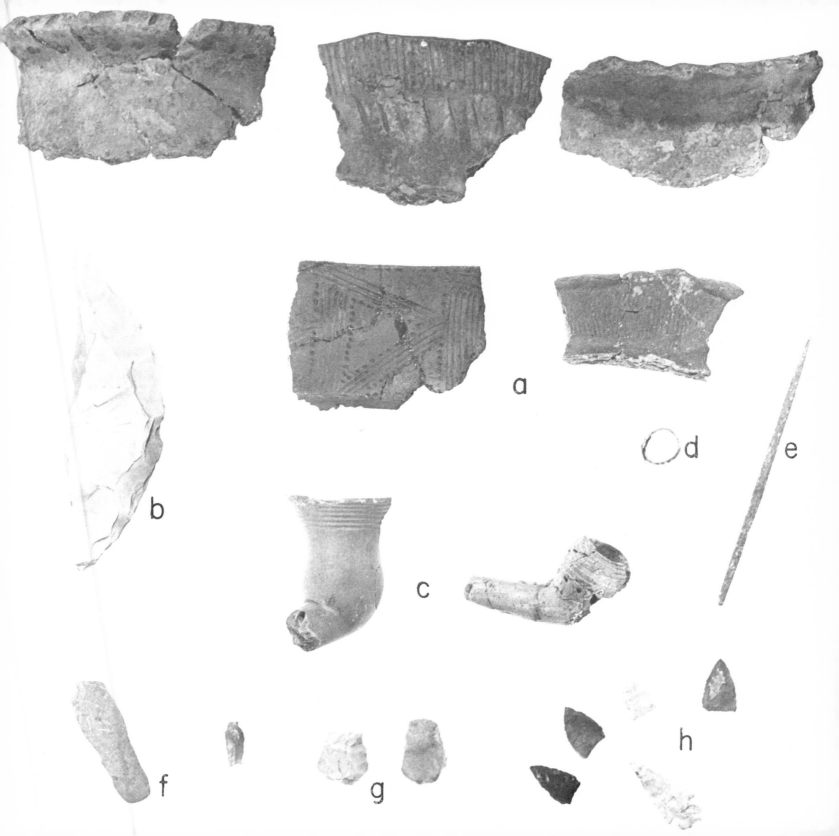

a

b

c

d

e

f

g

h

the western area

The Western area of Algonkian cultural development roughly encompasses the region running from western Lake Superior to the height of land separating the Hudson Bay drainage from the Great Lakes drainage, to southern Manitoba and the northern edge of Minnesota.

In this region a pottery tradition known as Blackduck prevails. Some archæologists believe that this particular pottery was made by the Assiniboine, a Siouian-speaking people closely related to the Yankton Sioux. I, on the other hand, believe that there is good archæological, ethnological, linguistic, and physical anthropological evidence that the Assiniboine move into southwestern Manitoba from Minnesota and North Dakota was a late event, even historic; and that the Blackduck pottery was developed by Algonkian-speaking people who had lived in the region from at least 900 A.D. and, in all likelihood, much earlier. There is some evidence that the Blackduck pottery evolved out of the preceding Laurel pottery of the Initial Woodland period. Another continuity with Laurel is the continuing construction of burial mounds. As with Laurel, these mounds are restricted to the region of the international boundary between Ontario and Minnesota as far east as the western end of Lake Superior.

The stone implements of the western Algonkians are very similar to those of the eastern Algonkians. The former group, however, had more ready access to the native copper deposits of western Lake Superior and copper awls, beads, bangles, and knives are relatively common. Stone smoking pipes appear as early as 950 A.D. and are shaped in a typical western style that has no relation to the pipe complex of the Iroquois peoples to the east. In the rare instances where bone has survived the acid northern soils, tools such as harpoons, beaver incisor knives, and awls, are common and the refuse bone consists mainly of fish and big game animals. Dog burials, similar to those found in eastern Algonkian sites, also occur. Human burials recovered from the mounds are generally found in a flexed position. Occasionally the skulls have been ritualistically treated, that is portions of the back of the skull have been removed and the eye sockets filled with clay, and shell beads

Fig. 5. Rock painting.

inserted for eyes. Another common trait is the placement of small clay mortuary vessels with the dead.

Although the Blackduck pottery is the dominant ceramic tradition found on western Algonkian sites, other pottery styles coming from the north, the south and the east also are generally present, suggesting that the female mobility noted for the eastern Algonkians also applies to the western bands. Blackduck pottery, on the other hand, has been found to the west in Saskatchewan, to the north on Hudson Bay, south into Michigan, and as far east as Lake Nipissing. As was the case with the eastern Algonkians, a number of western Algonkian sites containing European (French and English) trade goods have been excavated. The historic period is thus ushered in.

Plate 25. Western Algonkian artifacts.

Fig. a. Fragments from the rims of pottery vessels, referred to as Blackduck pottery.

Fig. b. Small pottery vessels specifically made for placement with the dead in burial mounds.

Fig. c. Stone smoking pipe—a wooden stem would have been inserted in the left end.

Fig. d. Stone amulet in the form of a beaver.

Fig. e. Arrowheads.

Fig. f. Scrapers.

Fig. g. Knife.

Fig. h. Antler harpoons.

Fig. i. Disc manufactured from a fragment of a pottery vessel. Such items are inferred to have functioned as tokens in some game and are referred to as gaming discs.

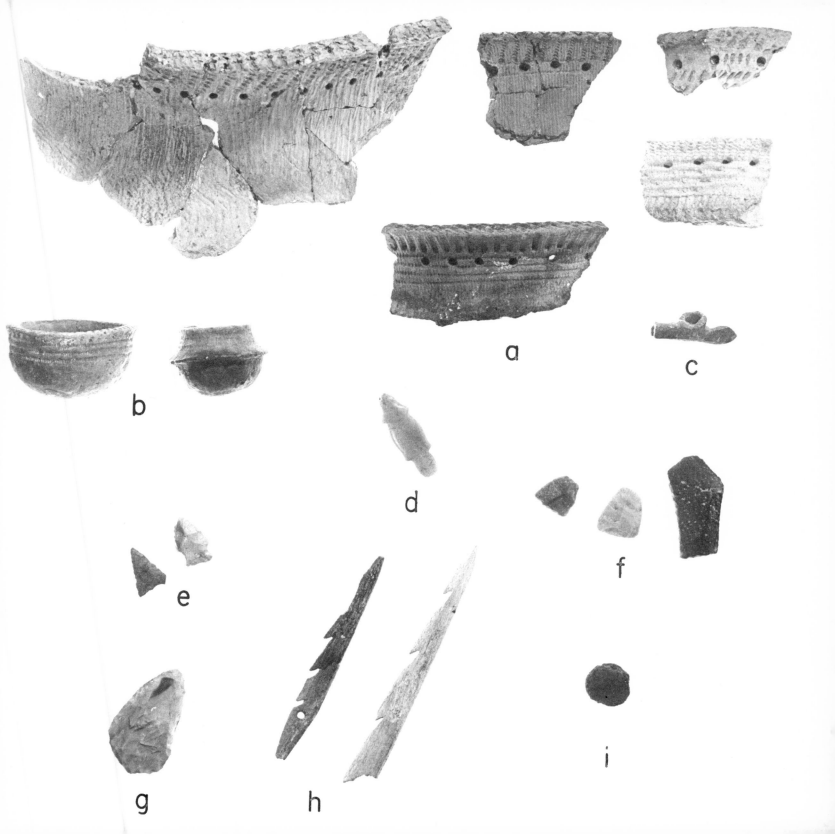

a

b

c

d

e

f

g

h

i

the northern area

The Northern area of Algonkian cultural development was basically centred in northern Manitoba but overlapped adjacent regions of Northern Ontario and Saskatchewan. In this area a pottery tradition known as Selkirk dominates. Most archæologists have regarded this pottery as being a product of the Cree. Its origins are unknown and it does not have any good antecedents in the earlier Laurel pottery of the Initial Woodland period. The Selkirk ceramic tradition produced bowls and plates in addition to pots. Despite their unique pottery, the northern Algonkians possessed basically the same kinds of stone and bone tools as their western and eastern kinsmen. They do appear, however, to have had a very close relationship with the western Algonkians and it is rare not to find some Blackduck pottery on a northern Algonkian site or, conversely, Selkirk pottery on a western Algonkian site. Again, the necessity to obtain wives from distant regions appears to offer the best explanation for this mixture of completely different pottery traditions.

In northern Manitoba the northern Algonkians have been traced from the historic period to the tenth century and in all likelihood a similar time depth exists for the related people who occupied northwestern Northern Ontario. This is approximately the same time depth as has been recorded for both the western and the eastern Algonkians. In both the Lac Seul area of Ontario and the north end of Lake Winnipeg in Manitoba, northern and western Algonkian sites have been found in close proximity to each other. It is not known at this early stage of investigation whether these sites were occupied at the same time or whether one group preceded the other into these regions.

Very little is yet known of the northern Algonkians of Ontario. What little information is available, supplemented by the evidence from Manitoba, suggests that these people are basically the same as the western Algonkians except that they developed a distinctive ceramic tradition. Their ceramics have been found as far east as the Ottawa Valley and in the area bordering on the north shore of Lake Superior.

If one ignored the pottery and considered only the stone and bone tools, the Eastern, Western and Northern Algonkian areas would be regarded as part of a single archæological complex. This impression is also reinforced by the general occurrence in isolated locations of rock paintings and boulder constructions, both of which probably served some occult religious function. The different pottery traditions have, however, been useful in dividing the enormous area of Northern Ontario into three rough geographic regions. The cultural and linguistic similarities seen among the present Algonkians of Northern Ontario are strongly reflected in their prehistory.

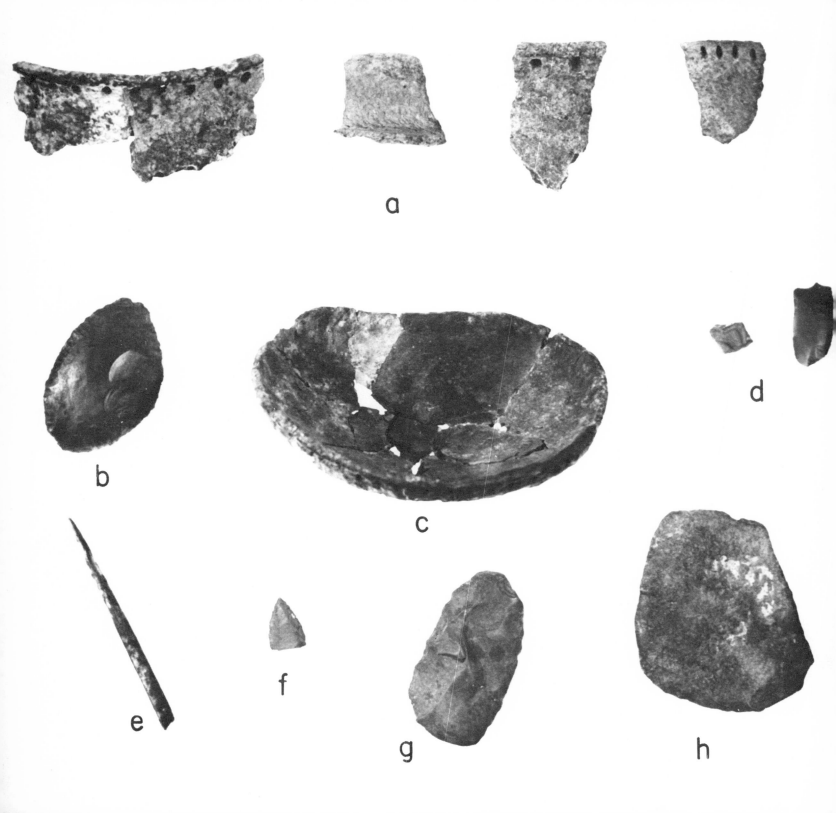

a

b

c

d

e

f

g

h

Plate 26. Northern Algonkian artifacts.

Fig. a. Fragments from the rims of typical pottery vessels. The roughened surface of these specimens results from impressing the wet clay with a twined fabric.

Fig. b. Stone knife.

Fig. c. Complete pottery bowl.

Fig. d. Stone scrapers.

Fig. e. Bone awl.

Fig. f. Arrowhead.

Fig. g. Flaked and ground axe.

Fig. h. Crude scraper form typical of Northern Algonkian culture.

Note: Most of the artifacts in this illustration came from northern Manitoba. Adequate Ontario specimens for illustration were not available in the collections of the National Museums. The artifacts shown, however, are representative of the types found in the northern portion of Northern Ontario, particularly that area adjacent to Manitoba.

Plate 27. Excavation of stratified Western Algonkian site on the north shore of Lake Superior. The lowermost black band, which represents an ancient living floor, has been dated by the radiocarbon method at 950 A.D. The uppermost living floor contained European trade items.

Fig. 6. Rock painting.

IV. Current Threat to the Preservation of Ontario Prehistory

With the coming of Europeans and written records the story of the native peoples of Ontario passes from prehistory to history. It should be pointed out, however, that more than 97 per cent of the time that man has occupied this province belongs to the dim and still largely unwritten pages of prehistory.

The introduction of European material culture, diseases, and intrigues drastically affected the cultures of Ontario's first citizens. The products of 11,000 years of human development, however, can never be completely destroyed. Many elements of the native cultures have become part of the average Canadian's life: corn, beans, and squash on the table and a smoke after supper; popcorn during the movie or perhaps some dessert topped with maple syrup. The canoe, toboggan, and snowshoe, are still common items in many households. These, however, are material things that are easily transferred from one culture to another just as the native blood that flows in many people's veins.

More difficult to assess and yet far more basic and resistant to change is the intellectual culture of people, the way they regard themselves and the world around them. In this area the least amount of communication has taken place between the native and the non-native occupants of the province. It is difficult to believe, however, that some of the attitudes and values developed over a period of 110 centuries, have not filtered, even though unconsciously, into the minds of at least some of the newcomers. Such a possibility cannot be demonstrated and it certainly cannot be measured.

What can be measured are the events involving the native people that have taken place in this province over the last 11,000 years. But for how long? The still unwritten pages of the province's and the nation's prehistory are disintegrating under an onslaught of flood waters, earth-moving machinery, and ignorance unparalleled for its intensity, efficiency, and inevitability. The nature of the problem is brutally simple. Any human or natural force that alters, buries, or floods the earth can be regarded as potentially destructive of archæological information. Against the massive forces of nature, industry, agriculture, urban expansion, and the vested material interests of the majority of Canadians are aligned the forces of archæology—a dozen archæologists and some sympathetic non-professionals.

The serious situation currently facing people concerned with the province's prehistory requires regional and individual efforts to be united in a common cause. Professional archæologists and non-professionals must cooperate. Provincial and federal agencies must cooperate. The citizens of Ontario must cooperate. This province has been blessed with a richness of natural resources, one of which is the natural record of our prehistory, a resource rapidly being destroyed by ignorance and indifference. It is a unique resource and once destroyed it can never be replaced. Action must be taken immediately to initiate, maintain and expand systems for both the retrieval and the preservation of this resource.

There are no alternatives and time is running out.

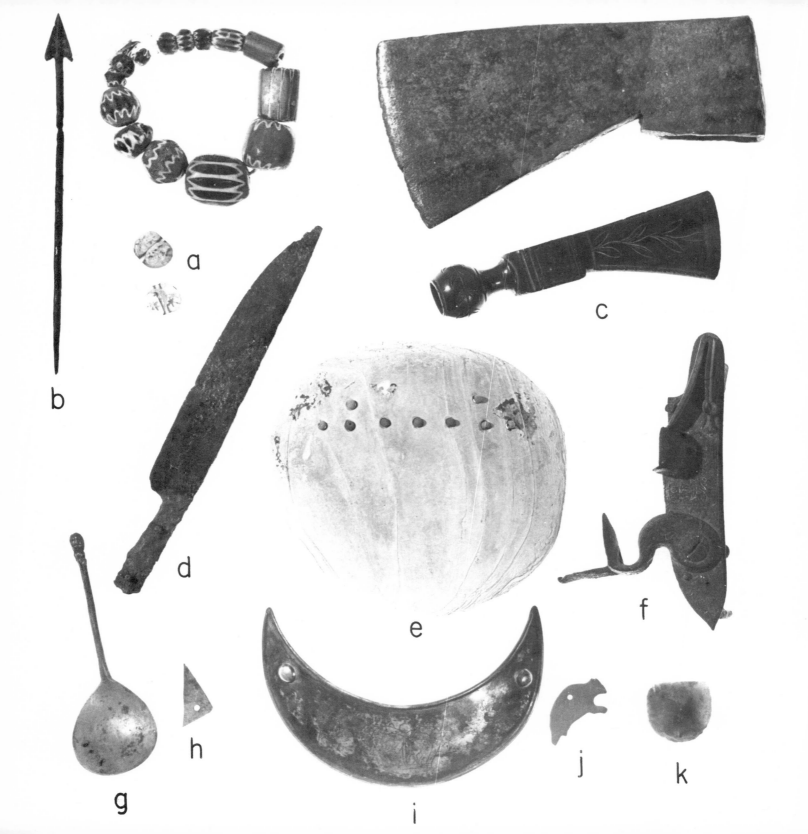

a

b

c

d

e

f

g

h

i

j

k

Plate 28. Historic period trade goods.

Fig. a. European trade beads typical of the French regime during the first half of the seventeenth century.

Fig. b. Iron spear head.

Fig. c. The upper iron axe belongs to the French period. The lower axe is an English period ceremonial brass axe with a pipe at the butt end that was smoked through the wooden axe handle which doubled as a pipe stem.

Fig. d. Iron knife.

Fig. e. Conch shell pendant with drilled holes that contain European glass beads.

Fig. f. French flintlock mechanism for a musket dated 1720 A.D.

Fig. g. Brass spoon of French origin.

Fig. h. Arrowhead made from a fragment of a copper trade kettle. Worn-out copper kettles were frequently cut up to manufacture beads, scrapers, and other items.

Fig. i. English silver-plated gorget.

Fig. j. Catlinite pendant made in the form of an animal. During the historic period this distinctive red stone from the west was widely traded into the east.

Fig. k. French gun flint.

appendix Archæological Agencies

What can the average citizen do who is concerned with preserving the province's prehistoric heritage? If he has knowledge of archæological collections or prehistoric village sites and, in particular, if he knows of archæological sites in danger of destruction, he could so inform one of the following university departments or museums.

Hamilton region

Department of Sociology and
Anthropology,
McMaster University,
Hamilton, Ontario.

London region

Department of Museums,
Room 30, Middlesex College,
University of Western Ontario,
London, Ontario.

Department of Anthropology,
University of Western Ontario,
London, Ontario.

Ottawa region

Archæological Survey of Canada,
Salvage Section,
National Museum of Man,
Ottawa, Ontario.

Peterborough region

Department of Anthropology,
Trent University,
Peterborough, Ontario.

Thunder Bay region

Department of Sociology and
Anthropology,
Lakehead University
Postal Station P,
Thunder Bay, Ontario.

Toronto region

Department of Anthropology,
University of Toronto,
Toronto, Ontario.

Office of the Chief Archæologist,
Royal Ontario Museum,
100 Queen's Park,
Toronto, Ontario.

Waterloo-Kitchener region

Department of Sociology and
Anthropology,
University of Waterloo,
Waterloo, Ontario.

Graduate Studies and University
Research,
Waterloo Lutheran University,
Waterloo, Ontario.

For those individuals who may wish to become more actively involved in Ontario archæology, it is recommended that they become members of the Ontario Archæological Society. The Ontario Archæological Society publishes a journal *Ontario Archæology* and a newsletter *Arch Notes.* In addition, the society holds monthly meetings, runs a fall excavation on an archæological site, and its members are quite often involved in the summer excavations of various provincial institutions. All inquiries concerning the society, membership in the society, and issues of past publications should be directed to the Corresponding Secretary, whose address can be obtained from an agency in the foregoing list.

suggested reading list

The following recommended readings in Ontario prehistory have been separately listed for Southern and Northern Ontario and have also been segregated by time period and cultural group.

In a number of instances where publications directly referring to the province are not available, reports from adjacent provinces or states are recommended, as they reflect a basically similar cultural development. An attempt has been made to list only reports that have a broad scope or that present a detailed examination of a major archæological site.

The bibliography is not only restricted but is somewhat erratic in its specific coverage. Numerous pertinent references, however, can be readily obtained from bibliographies included in the recommended books and articles.

General
Southern Ontario
Kennedy, Clyde C.
(1970). *The Upper Ottawa Valley.* Pembroke, Renfrew County Council.
Contains a brief and well illustrated outline of the local prehistory, from the Laurentian Archaic to the Iroquois and Algonkian.

Kenyon, Walter A.
(1957). The Inverhuron site. *Royal Ont. Museum, Art and Archæology Occasional Paper* 1.
Description of a site on Lake Huron containing Archaic period to Iroquois occupations.

Ritchie, William A.
(1965). *The archæology of New York State.* New York, Natural Hist. Press. A detailed study beginning with the Palæo-Indian period and ending with the historic Iroquois. Many of the developments that took place in New York prehistory are basically similar to developments in Southern Ontario.

Northern Ontario
Ridley, Frank
(1954). The Frank Bay site, Lake Nipissing, Ontario. *Amer. Antiquity* 20: (1).
Description of a site containing Shield Archaic to historic Algonkian occupations.

Wright, J.V.
(1963). An archæological survey along the north shore of Lake Superior. *National Museum of Can. Anthropology Papers* 3.
A short general statement beginning with the Palæo-Indian period (Plano) and ending with the Terminal Woodland period (Algonkian).
(1968). The Boreal Forest (prehistory of Hudson Bay). In *Science, history and Hudson Bay,* eds. C.S. Beals and D.A. Shenstone, vol. 1. Ottawa, Dept. of Energy, Mines and Resources.
A general description of the prehistory of the forested region flanking Hudson Bay.

Palæo-Indian period
General
MacDonald, George F.
(1968). Debert, a Palæo-Indian site in central Nova Scotia. *National Museums of Can. Anthropology Papers* 16.
A detailed description of a Palæo-Indian period (Clovis) site.

Northern Ontario
Lee, Thomas E.
(1957). The antiquity of the Sheguiandah site. *Can. Field Naturalist* 71: (3).

A description of a Palæo-Indian period to Archaic period quarry site on Manitoulin Island.

MacNeish, Richard S.
(1952). A possible early site in the Thunder Bay District, Ontario. *National Museum of Can. Bulletin* 126.
A description of a Palæo-Indian period (Plano) quarry site on the north shore of Lake Superior.

Archaic Period
Southern Ontario
Johnston, Richard B.
(1968). Archæology of Rice Lake, Ontario. *National Museums of Can. Anthropology Papers* 19. Description of Laurentian Archaic and later materials.

Kennedy, Clyde C.
(1966). Preliminary report on the Morrison's Island-6 site. *National Museum of Can. Bulletin* 206, pp. 100-125.
A description of a Laurentian Archaic village site and cemetery in adjacent Quebec.

Northern Ontario
Ridley, Frank
(1966). Archæology of Lake Abitibi, Ontario-Quebec. *Anthropological Journal of Can.* 4:(2).
Description of a number of sites, mostly Shield Archaic but also including Initial and Terminal Woodland components.

Wright, J.V.
(In press). The Shield Archaic. *National Museums of Can. Publications in Archæology* 3.
Detailed description of the Shield Archaic.

Initial Woodland Period
Southern Ontario
Johnston, Richard B.
(1968). The archæology of the Serpent Mounds site. *Royal Ont. Museum, Art and Archæology Occasional Paper* 10.
Detailed examination of a large ceremonial and village site of the Point Peninsula culture.

Levesque, René, F. Fitz Osborne, J.V. Wright
(1964). Le gisement de Batiscan. *Musée national du Canada, Études anthropologiques* 6.

A report on a Meadowood culture village site.

Spence, Michael W.
(1967). A Middle Woodland burial complex in the St. Lawrence Valley. *National Museums of Can. Anthropology Papers* 14.

Spence, Michael W. and J. Russell Harper
(1968). The Cameron's Point site. *Royal Ont. Museum, Art and Archæology Occasional Paper* 12.
Description of a Point Peninsula culture village and burial site.

Wright, J.V.
(1967). The Laurel tradition and the Middle Woodland period. *National Museums of Can. Bulletin* 217.
Detailed description of the Laurel culture and its Initial Woodland period neighbours.

Wright, J.V. and J.E. Anderson
(1963). The Donaldson site. *National Museum of Can. Bulletin* 184.
Detailed description of the archæology and physical anthropology of a Saugeen culture site.

Terminal Woodland Period

General

Wright, J.V.

(1968). The application of the direct historical approach to the Iroquois and the Ojibwa. *Ethnohistory* 15: (1).

Iroquois (Huron-Petun) and Ojibwa culture history is traced from the historic period to 900 A.D.

Southern Ontario (Ontario Iroquois)

Emerson, J.N.

(1956). *Understanding Iroquois pottery in Ontario.* Toronto, Archæological Society. An introduction to the use of pottery by archæologists to reconstruct Iroquois culture.

(1966). The Payne site: an Iroquoian manifestation in Prince Edward County, Ontario. *National Museum of Can. Bulletin* 206, pp. 126-257.

A description of an Iroquois site with clearly explained methods of artifact analysis.

Kenyon, Walter A.

(1968). The Miller site. *Royal Ont. Museum, Art and Archæology Occasional Paper* 14.

Description of a twelfth-century palisaded Pickering culture site.

MacNeish, Richard S.

(1952). Iroquois pottery types. *National Museum of Can. Bulletin* 124.

The original study that demonstrated the local development of Iroquois culture in its historic homeland based upon the use of pottery types. A synthesis of general Iroquois cultural development.

Ridley, Frank

(1961). *Archæology of the Neutral Indians.* Islington, Ont., Etobicoke Hist. Society.

A study of the Neutral Iroquois based upon excavation and information from private collections.

Trigger, Bruce G.

(1970). The strategy of Iroquoian prehistory. *Ont. Archæology* 14.

An historical examination of the various theories of Iroquois origins.

White, Marian E.

(1961). Iroquois culture history in the Niagara frontier area of New York state. *Univ. of Mich. Anthropological Papers* 16.

A detailed study of a number of village sites belonging to the Neutral-Erie cultural development.

Wintemberg, W.J.
(1928). Uren prehistoric village site, Oxford County, Ontario. *National Museum of Can. Bulletin* 51.
A detailed examination of an early fourteenth-century Iroquois village site.
(1939). Lawson prehistoric village site, Middlesex County, Ontario. *National Museum of Can. Bulletin* 94.
A detailed examination of a mid-sixteenth century Neutral Iroquois village site.
(1946). The Sidney-Mackay village site. *Amer. Antiquity* 11: (3).
A detailed examination of an early historic Petun village site.
(1948). The Middleport prehistoric village site. *National Museum of Can. Bulletin* 109.
A detailed examination of an early fifteenth-century Iroquois site.

Wright, J.V.
(1966). The Ontario Iroquois tradition. *National Museum of Can. Bulletin* 210.
A general synthesis of the prehistoric development of the Huron-Petun and the Neutral-Erie.

Wright, J.V. and **J.E. Anderson**
(1969). The Bennett site. *National Museums of Can. Bulletin* 229.
A detailed study of the archæology and physical anthropology of a late Pickering culture site.

Southern Ontario
(St. Lawrence Iroquois)
Pendergast, James F.
(1966). Three prehistoric Iroquois components in eastern Ontario. *National Museum of Can. Bulletin* 208.
A detailed examination of three St. Lawrence Iroquois sites.

Wintemberg, W.J.
(1936). The Roebuck prehistoric village site, Grenville County, Ontario. *National Museum of Can. Bulletin* 83.
A detailed examination of a St. Lawrence Iroquois site.

Northern Ontario
MacNeish, Richard S.
(1958). An introduction to the archæology of southeast Manitoba. *National Museum of Can. Bulletin* 157.
A study ranging from the Archaic period to the Terminal Woodland period but of pertinence to adjacent northern Ontario.

Wright, J.V.
(1965). A regional examination of Ojibwa culture history. *Anthropologica, n.s.* 7: (2).
An attempt to trace Algonkian culture history back to 900 A.D.
(1966). The Pic River site. *National Museum of Can. Bulletin* 206, pp. 54-99.
A detailed examination of a western Algonkian site.
(1968a). The Michipicoten site, Ontario. *National Museums of Can. Bulletin* 224, pp. 1-85.
A detailed examination of an eastern Algonkian site.
(1968b). Cree culture history in the southern Indian Lake region. *National Museums of Can. Bulletin* 232, pp. 1-31.
An examination of northern Algonkian sites in Manitoba with pertinence to northern Ontario.

Historic Period
General
Kinietz, W. Vernon
(1940). The Indians of the western Great Lakes, 1615-1760. *Occasional Contributions from the Museum of Anthropology of the Univ. of Mich.* 10.

Thwaites, Reuben Gold, ed.
(1896-1901). *Jesuit Relations and allied documents.* 73 vols. Cleveland, Burrows Bros.

Southern Ontario
Cartier, Jacques
(1924). *The voyages of Jacques Cartier.* Ed. H.P. Biggar. Publications of the Public Archives of Canada, no. 11. Ottawa.

Champlain, Samuel de
(1922-36). *The works of Samuel de Champlain.* Ed. H.P. Biggar. Toronto, Champlain Society.

Jones, Arthur Edward
(1909). «8endaken ehen» or Old Huronia. *5th Report of the Bureau of Archives, Prov. of Ont. 1908.*

Sagard-Théodat, Gabriel
(1939). *The long journey to the country of the Hurons.* Ed. G.M. Wrong. Toronto, Champlain Society.

Tooker, Elisabeth
(1964). An ethnography of the Huron Indians, 1615-1649. *Smithsonian Inst. Bureau of Amer. Ethnology Bulletin* 190. Washington, D.C.

Trigger, Bruce G.
(1969). *The Huron farmers of the north.* New York, Holt, Rinehart and Winston.

Miscellaneous
Rock Paintings and Problematical Structures

Dewdney, Selwin and **Kenneth E. Kidd**
(1962). *Indian rock paintings of the Great Lakes.* Toronto, pub. for the Quetico Foundation by Univ. Toronto Press.

Noble, W.C.
(1968). Vision pits, cairns, and petroglyphs at Rock Lake, Algonquin Provincial Park, Ontario. *Ont. Archæology* 11.

Radiocarbon Dates
Wilmeth, Roscoe
(1969). Canadian archæological radiocarbon dates. *National Museums of Can. Bulletin* 232, pp. 68-127.
Contains a current list of all archæological radiocarbon dates in Ontario as well as the rest of the country.

Physical Anthropology
Anderson, J.E.
(1963). The people of Fairty. *National Museum of Can. Bulletin* 193, pp. 28-129.
A detailed physical anthropological study of a late fourteenth-century Huron ossuary.
(1968). The Serpent Mounds site physical anthropology. *Royal Ont. Museum, Art and Archæology Occasional Paper* 11.
A detailed physical anthropological study of both Initial and Terminal Woodland burials from the Serpent Mounds site.